RENARD THE FOX

Renard the Fox

Translated from the Old French
by Patricia Terry

UNIVERSITY OF CALIFORNIA PRESS
Berkeley • Los Angeles • London

University of California Press
Berkeley and Los Angeles, California
University of California Press, Ltd.
London, England

Designer, David Ford

Originally published by
Northeastern University Press
First California Printing 1992
Copyright © 1983 by Patricia Terry

The preparation of this volume was made possible (in part) by a
grant from the Translation Program of the National Endowment for
the Humanities, an independent federal agency.

Library of Congress Cataloging in Publication Data

Roman de Renart. English
  Renard the Fox / translated from the Old French by Patricia Terry.
    p. cm.
  Translation of: Roman de Renart.
  Includes bibliographical references.
  ISBN 0-520-07683-4 (cloth).—ISBN 0-520-07684-2 (pbk.)
    1. Reynard the Fox (Legendary character)—Poetry.   2. Animals—
Poetry.   I. Terry, Patricia Ann, 1929–   . II. Title.
[PQ1508.E5T47 1992]
841'.1—dc20   91-23051
                                                          CIP

Manufactured in the United States of America

This book is a print-on-demand volume. It is manufactured
using toner in place of ink. Type and images may be less
sharp than the same material seen in traditionally printed
University of California Press editions.

The paper used in this publication meets the minimum
requirements of ANSI/NISO Z39.48-1992(R
1997)(Permanence of Paper)

For Robert
Sine Qua Non

ACKNOWLEDGMENTS

It is very pleasant to conclude a project by thanking those who participated in its beginning or furthered its progress. I am particularly indebted to Mary Ann Caws for initial encouragement and support, and also to Frederick Goldin; to Joan Ferrante for having brought her scholarship and wit to the task of being Official Reader; to Patricia Stirnemann of the Bibliothèque Nationale. I am very grateful to have been allowed to explore that library's manuscripts of *Le Roman de Renart* and to reproduce in this book illuminations from Fonds français 115, 1579, 1580, 1581, 12583, and 12584.

To the National Endowment for the Humanities and to its advisers who recommended this translation, I wish to express my gratitude for their having made available to me the time in which to undertake it. It is very gratifying to have my first publisher (*Poems of Jules LaForgue*) reissue *Renard the Fox*. I want particularly to thank its acquisitions editor Doris Kretschmer for all the time and energy she devoted to the project.

Contents

RENARD THE FOX

Introduction

By the middle of the thirteenth century in France, the common word for fox, *goupil*, had been replaced by the name of the fox whose adventures are related here. Nothing could better demonstrate the popular appeal of the *Roman de Renart* and its anti-establishment attitudes. The authors were anything but pedantic; nor were they out to write the simple tales for children extracted from their work by later bowdlerizers. They attacked, with gusto and a subterranean idealism, the government of their country, its legal system, its Church, the formalities of feudalism, the hollow protection offered the underprivileged, and the unredeemed brutality of peasants. They put us on the side of a revolutionary individual who is, however, no social reformer but a murderer and a thief. These writers have their own *renardie*, craftiness and guile, and take full advantage of the fact that at a masquerade, if the rhymes are good enough, almost anything can be said.

Unlike the fables from which the animal characters partly derive, the *Roman de Renart* has no overt moral purpose. No doubt it is intended to be instructive, but the more it exposes the complex weaknesses that constitute the very fabric of the society it depicts, the more it makes them an occasion for enjoyment. When the characters are clothed in real fur and real feathers, not only is their experience of life, insofar as it resembles our own, an entertainment, but there is further charm in those moments when we are reminded, by a gesture of wing or tail, that they *are* animals. The same literary mechanism, however, holds bleak implications. Laws, even those of a king, cannot really protect the vulnerable creatures in the *Roman*, because predation is an irreproachable norm of animal existence. To think of Renard as a fox makes rich comedy of his trial and condemnation for murdering a chicken. However, since Renard is one of King Noble's most important vassals, the reader might infer that the predations of a *seigneur* would similarly be part of the very nature of the beast.

The title *Roman de Renart* was applied in the late twelfth century to a loosely organized collection of tales in the vernacular whose principal characters were a fox and a wolf. These verse narratives were written independently of each other and are referred to as *branches* by some of the authors. Approximately fifteen tales were written between 1174 and 1205, and production of related stories, lacking in quality if not in enthusiasm, continued until the middle of the thirteenth century. All the branches are derived, directly or indirectly, from the work of Pierre de Saint-Cloud, who was the first to write in French of the famous triangle consisting of Renard the fox, Ysengrin the wolf, and Hersent his wife, which forms the nucleus of the major adventures. Pierre did not invent the hostility of fox and wolf, but he did give the wolf a less than virtuous wife, a fact that complicates matters when Renard is eventually brought to trial, accused by Hersent and Ysengrin of rape. That episode is narrated in detail by the most brilliant of the Renard authors in "The Trial of Renard." These oldest sections of the *Roman* are completed, in the present translation, by "Renard's Pilgrimage," written between 1180 and 1200, which describes Renard in his not very mellow old age.

References to the *Roman de Renart* in the twelfth century and throughout the thirteenth century—in epic poems, romances, chronicles, sermons, and countless edifying and unedifying stories—more than justify Lucien Foulet's statement that few if any works of the period were so widely read.[1] For literary monuments of similar significance one would have to refer to *Tristan et Iseut* and *Le Roman de la Rose*, certainly superior to *Le Roman de Renart* in dignity but appealing to a much more restricted public. For generations of readers, including Chaucer, the French authors established the archetype of the rogue fox, but the very popularity of the source was responsible for its virtual disappearance. The best and oldest branches were buried in the avalanche of derivative works—some 25,000 lines copied and recopied in conflicting, contradictory manuscripts in which the outlines of the individual tales were obscured and sometimes vanished entirely. The Renard stories survived through foreign adaptations, particularly the late twelfth century German *Reinhart Fuchs*, by Henri Glichczâre; a fourteenth century Flemish version is the source of what medieval material remains in Goethe's *Reineke Fuchs*.

The earliest extant French manuscripts are thirteenth century copies. The first modern edition was made by D. M. Méon in 1826. Ernest Martin's more rigorously edited text first appeared in 1882. The present translation is based on this text as reprinted and emended in 1970. The text of another manuscript was published, beginning in 1948, by Mario Roques. Known as the Cangé manuscript, it contains some interesting variations of the texts used here, as indicated in the notes.

A number of theories have developed about the sources of the *Roman*, many of them inspired by the work of the nineteenth-century philologist Jakob Grimm (author of *Grimm's Fairy Tales*). Grimm's studies placed the origins of the *Roman* in the depths of German forests where observations of animal life would have given rise to a folklore transformed, many centuries later, into the medieval poems. The considerable body of opinion, pro and con, evoked by Grimm had subsided with no victory on either side when, in 1892, Leopold Sudre dissected the *Roman* into its thematic elements—the bear's weakness for honey, the vanity of the cock, and so on—and demonstrated that comparable episodes can be found from Sanskrit to Swedish.

Subsequent criticism, most notably that of Lucien Foulet, has convincingly established that there is no need to go so far, at least to identify the sources of the French text. The decades immediately preceding the first appearance of the *Roman* (in about 1170–1175, according to Foulet's chronology) offered a considerable number of possible literary antecedents, notably Marie de France's translations of Aesop's fables and Nivard's Latin poem *Ysengrimus* (c. 1150). Foulet believes that Pierre de Saint-Cloud probably knew them both (p. 151). Pierre's reading of *Ysengrimus* is virtually certain and would have been far more significant. The Latin poem seems to have supplied the idea of an animal epic organized around the conflict of fox and wolf.

Ysengrimus, however, is a complex and very erudite clerical work, exceedingly long-winded. Resemblances between it and the *Roman de Renart* involve the plot alone. Foulet (p. 150) points out that the curious family relationships between the animals of Branch II are already established in *Ysengrimus*, in which Reinardus is not only the cock's *compère (compater)* but also his cousin and the nephew of Ysengrimus. Reinardus and Renard meet their intended victims in the same order. In *Ysengrimus*, the mistreatment of the wolf cubs occurs at the beginning of the fox's visit to their home, and nothing about it is contradicted by either Renard's character or the plot. In the *Roman* the motive is quite obscure, and one would be inclined to agree with Foulet (p. 136) that it shows the author somewhat ill at ease with his predecessor's version of the episode.

Pierre de Saint-Cloud's account of this adventure differs from that of Nivard on a point of such capital importance that it influences the entire story; in the Old French version the wolf's wife more or less initiates the adultery and

certainly welcomes it. This suggests a possible explanation
for the author's having retained Renard's mistreatment
of Hersent's cubs. The plot must somehow proceed to rape,
a difficult problem if Hersent was so readily seduced. The
rage of the cubs makes them refuse to keep Hersent's
secret from her husband, and she can defend herself only
by pretending to be furious with Renard. She actually
seems to become so, perhaps simply under the influence
of adrenaline; she outdistances Ysengrin in pursuing the
fox and so plunges headlong into the excessively narrow
entrance to his lair. After that, her desire for vengeance
is quite natural, and the occasion offers a particularly good
example of Renard's gratuitous wickedness.

Pierre's narrative continues in the branch called Va,[2]
but another author completed Pierre's work five years later
by bringing Renard to trial. Renard is condemned to go
on a pilgrimage, at his own insincere suggestion, but he
actually starts out only in Branch VIII. These branches
(II, Va, I, and VIII) are translated in this book, presented
in the coherent order. Branch I clearly refers to its predecessor, giving us Pierre's name.[3] These are the oldest
and best poems in the collection, and they fully justify
Bossuat's statement that the *Roman de Renart* provides
us with the most faithful image we have of feudal society
at its zenith.[4]

Based on these early texts of the *Roman* alone, an eval-
uation of the French monarchy in the late twelfth century
would be quite accurate. The supremacy of the king is
recognized by all. He even has the power to declare a
universal truce (as Louis VII had actually done in 1155).[5]
The greater and lesser vassals attend his court, where a
respectful decorum is maintained. Although none of the
vassals has the strength of King Noble the lion, there are
some, like the wolf, who have a great position at court
and who are always threatening to flout the law if it cannot
be adjusted to suit them. There is constant danger of

alliances that might be able to influence or attack the king. On the other hand, as even Renard's behavior occasionally shows, King Noble has a genuine prestige; the respect he inspires goes to a certain extent beyond his ability to command it.

The project of a universal peace both in the *Roman* and in actuality is more than ambitious. Private wars were prohibited by *L'Enquête de Caen* in 1091, and they had to be prohibited again early in the thirteenth century in the *Très Ancienne Coutume de Normandie*.[6] King Louis's general truce was in force for ten years, but in practice his experience may have resembled that of King Noble, who discovers that the strong continue to devour the weak when hunger and opportunity coincide. For the most part, references to the truce in the *Roman de Renart* are either hypocritical or jocular. The ultimate answer to disobedience is, of course, war. The great lord, so threatened, retires to his fortress, as Renard does to Maupertuis, lays in supplies, and has a good chance of wearing out and even harassing the opposition. Branch Ia relates exactly this situation, but unfortunately in a style without much literary quality.

The king's court as seen in the *Roman* is primarily judicial. Hersent and Ysengrin are as sure as is Pinte the hen that the king will give them a fair judgment and a legal way to avenge their wrongs. King Noble, exactly in the manner of Charlemagne in *La Chanson de Roland*, appoints a council to meet and decide on an appropriate verdict—great lords were normally judged by their peers. Regardless of whether the council's decision would necessarily be binding on the king, he does ask for advice, turning to the learned jurist from Lombardy as well, and for the most part follows it.

The council's deliberations stand as proof that the authors of the *Roman* were not invariably pessimistic about human nature. Bricemer the stag and Baucent the boar are both absolutely on Ysengrin's side, but that does not prevent them from judging Hersent's testimony inadmissible since, as Bricemer says, she is inclined to do whatever her husband asks and is, besides, a very convincing liar. Baucent agrees that testimony from interested parties is not to be relied on and that the case cannot be decided until Renard himself appears before the court. Their friend Bruin's account of how Renard betrayed him does not change their opinion. Graven (p. 121) is surely correct in stating that although the guilty party escapes punishment in the *Roman*, justice at Noble's court is an ideal sincerely pursued. Nevertheless, the king reacts with an exclamation of pleasure when the council relieves him of further participation in Renard's trial. A noble's claim to innocence is to be proved by an oath taken in the presence of an esteemed watchdog (not an impartial observer, one would think, for a fox), and the king is very responsive to the suggestion that he himself will be unable to attend.[7]

Once a formal accusation has been made, the accused must be brought within reach of jurisdiction. The self-confident Renard does not bother attending the court at first, although it is a plenary session and no one else is absent. Nevertheless, in both Branch Va and Branch I, he obeys the king without coercion.

Legal custom as set down in the early-thirteenth-century *La Très Ancienne Coutume de Bretagne* considered failure to appear when summoned an admission of guilt.[8] Renard's attitude also contains, of course, an element of bravado. He is a distinguished vassal of the king, but his enemies at court are far more numerous than his friends. None would know better than he how thin the veneer of universal peace and deference to the law would become once he was really dependent on the truce and the law for protection. Against this reality stands the statement of the Lombard camel, clear despite his multilingual jargon: the primary duty of the king is to make sure that no one is condemned without trial or, when proved guilty, escapes without punishment. If he cannot maintain justice in his lands, ruling his vassals honorably and with affection, he might as well become a monk!

Very little is treated as sacred in the *Roman*, certainly not the clerical orders. Respect is paid to them, however, through their contribution to the plot. Renard more than once lures Ysengrin to disaster by promising him a share in the monks' rich stores of food. Apart from farmers and peasants, few of whom have significant speaking roles, the human characters in the *Roman* are monks and hermits. These may be credulous enough to be helpful, like the friar Renard meets in Branch II who is persuaded that Renard is merely having a friendly race with the dogs, or dangerous, like the parish priest of Branch I, father of Martin de la Tour, who stuck a manure fork into Bruin's side (although the priest appears much less effective later when he leaps half-naked out of his unsanctified bed to attack Tibert and lose the battle).

The hermit who listens to Renard's confession in Branch VIII is more convincing in his spiritual role, but the case, he says, is beyond his powers. The exercise of priestly functions is not limited to the ordained. Bruin puts on a stole and presides at Mme. Copee's funeral. Grinbert the badger not only listens to Renard's confession but gives him absolution in both French and Latin. Renard, in any case, loves to confess: it provides an opportunity for dwelling on moments of past triumph.

In the absence of conclusive evidence, or in deference to a vassal powerful enough to prefer God's judgment to man's, combat or trial by ordeal was a familiar procedure. It had, of course, its problems. Hersent suggests the most extreme demonstrations of her innocence, offering, for instance, to carry a red-hot iron. Noble is all in favor, but Ysengrin realizes that not only his wife's hands but his pride would be at risk. The council's decision in Renard's case is that he should simply swear to his innocence in the presence of his accuser and a reliable judge. The insistence on there being a holy relic to swear on seems to come only from Ysengrin; certainly Bricemer thinks that Renard's word alone would be sufficient. Neither he nor anyone else, however, questions the elevation of Roenel to sainthood simply by reason of his supposed death, nor do they admit to any difference between an ordeal that involves physical danger and one that, at least in principle, does not.

Not only instant sainthood but miracle working and instant martyrdom occur in the *Roman*, both in fact engineered by Ysengrin and his ally the dog. Ysengrin is cured of earache by putting his head on the grave of Renard's victim Mme. Copee, with Roenel as witness to reinforce the faith one should have in holy miracles. Although it is usual to say that Ysengrin is stupid—certainly he is no match for Renard in unscrupulous cleverness—this ploy cannot be faulted as a means of intensifying public outcry against the killer (Branch I, lines 459–469).

When Renard succeeds in having his sentence of death commuted to a lifelong pilgrimage, the lion asks the fox to forgive them all, and Queen Fiere says, ''We'll pray for you, / And remember us in your prayers too'' (Branch I, lines 1441–1442). Expressions of Christian charity and piety are rare enough in the poems to deserve mention, but these are, of course, quickly followed by a response not at all in kind. The authors of ''The Trial of Renard'' and ''Renard's Pilgrimage'' express the opinion that those who undertake journeys to the Holy Land are likely to return worse than when they started out. This is why King Noble does not want Renard ever to return, even presumably edified by his visits to holy shrines. Renard, with the same excuse, decides later in life that plans for reform are best carried out at home.

Although direct comments from the author are rare in the *Roman*, there is at least one evocation of court life from a strictly human point of view. The speech is given to Renard but has little relevance except as a personal complaint from the poet. In ''The Trial of Renard,'' Renard explains that he wanted to enjoy a good dinner before going to court, for fear that he would be treated as a poor man once he got there (lines 505–530). There is a wonderfully vivid description of the unfortunate guest fighting off the housedogs who crowd around him since he has no place at the table and making his one drink and single serving last as long as possible. Renard himself, who could claim to be Noble's most distinguished vassal, would certainly have been better treated. The author seems not to be imagining special circumstances owing to Renard's fall from grace, but rather expressing grievances of his own. The most acerbic comments are directed at thieving seneschals and cooks, the implication being that the lords of castles would be more generous were they not deprived of the means.

The other authors of the early branches remain more detached, their interventions tending to be briefer and more conventional, but they, like the author of Branch I, express themselves indirectly through literary allusions— references to books, stylistic echoes, or resemblances between the animal characters and the humans of other fiction. This, of course, adds both depth and humor to the characterization. Renard may be either Roland or the traitor Ganelon, depending on whether we are admiring his courage or deploring his motives. King Noble sometimes recalls Charlemagne, sitting on his throne surrounded by respectful warriors, and sometimes the less heroic figure of King Arthur as he appears in the romances of Chrétien de Troyes.

There are echoes of Guinevere in Queen Fiere's gracious attitude toward Renard, and this conjures up Lancelot as an image of all that Renard is not. Hersent parodies Iseut, especially when she clamors for trial by ordeal and contrives statements of the truth that will communicate, under oath, an opposite meaning (Branch I, lines 147–150). Ysengrin, like King Mark, vacillates between crude ferocity and a readiness to believe what he wants to no matter how flimsy the evidence. The evocation of literary grandeur is a comment on the unredeemed adulteries of actual life as the *Roman* presents it.

Hersent may have eloquence and infidelity in common with Iseut, but her lover is scarcely Tristan. Encounters with other creatures are, for Renard, so many opportunities to prove himself their superior. His mistreatment of titmouse, cat, and crow persuade us that Hersent's embracing Renard on one occasion would not prevent her being raped by him when she was vulnerable to attack. Neither scruples nor self-interest restrain him; he sees no advantage in making alliances with beings inferior to him in either wit or physical power. Consequently, once outside the shelter of Maupertuis, he is in enemy territory, and the larger the number joined against him in their righteous indignation, the more both his contempt and his courage increase. In his total alienation from society, and in his awareness of it, he becomes at certain moments the first of the Romantic heroes. To Tibert, summoning him to face the court's sure condemnation, Renard replies (Branch I, lines 793–795):

> How I deal with threats you shall see,
> And those who'd sharpen their teeth on me.
> While I can I will live my life!

When Renard stands before King Noble at last, his first concern is not to conciliate but to remind the king of his services (unlike Roland he does not enumerate them). If Bruin and Tibert came to harm, it was owing to their own weaknesses. "Who ate the honey, if not the bear?" How could Renard possibly have caused injury to such an enormous fellow? Unfortunately, King Noble, seeing Renard primarily as the murderer of Mme. Copee, is not in a mood for making nice distinctions, and Renard soon finds himself about to be hanged. Even in despair he fights on, appealing to the king's religious scruples, until he is saved. As a penitent he puts just enough distance between himself and the court so that, standing on a hilltop above them, he can use his pilgrim's flag to express his absolute disdain for those he has gulled, risking his life for the gesture once again.

Renard's defense—that Tibert and Bruin were trapped by their own greed—is perfectly true as far as it goes. Beyond it, however, is Renard's unabashed enjoyment of their suffering. Thus Grinbert reproaches Renard when he brings him the king's letter (Branch I, lines 982–984):

> What did you want of Ysengrin?
> Why harm Tibert? Why hurt Bruin?
> You have betrayed them to your ruin.

Renard does not answer these questions directly, but he clearly does not regard them as irrelevant. This same devilish trait is established in Branch II by Renard's unprovoked attack on Hersent's cubs and then on their mother. In earlier scenes, the titmouse was supposed to be both relative and friend. In Tiecelin's case Renard could have contented himself with the cheese alone. He had absolutely nothing to gain from attempting to trap Tibert, a good fighter who had, just a moment before, signed on as the fox's ally.

But we delight in all these adventures, just as we enjoy the incongruous eloquence of the hens even as we sympathize with their bereavement, and so participate in a characteristically ambivalent medieval approach to reality (thanks to which God, at least in romances, protects illicit lovers). Renard reformed would not be Renard. When we encounter him, older and grayer, in Branch VIII, it seems at first that he is genuinely unhappy about the hatred he inspires. When they realize that he really is lamenting his inability to perform reprehensible deeds, most readers will be inclined to feel more sympathy than regret. The pilgrimage makes it clear that Renard can still lead the unsuspecting into peril, again with the excuse, if one be needed, that their own weakness led them to it. The sheep and the donkey insist on having a roof over their heads, and Renard doesn't feel obliged to say that the lodging he proposes belongs to the wolf.

Renard at home is someone else again. At Maupertuis, wonderfully poised between baronial castle and fox's lair, Renard lives a domestic life of considerable charm. He has a devoted wife, always ready to bind up his wounds, prepare his bath, and soothe him with an invalid's meal. We see her, accompanied by their three sons, hurrying to embrace Renard when he escapes the pursuing horde at the end of Branch I. Hermeline, unlike the wolf's wife, is completely faithful to her spouse as long as she thinks he is alive. (Branch Ib, which relates her erroneous widowhood and attempt at remarriage, concludes with a quick return to domestic harmony.) About to leave for his trial, Renard embraces his wife and children and explains to his sons how they can be safe in their castle, at least for quite a while. He commends them to God and then speaks a prayer for himself which is a striking example of his unflinching insight (Branch I, lines 1129–1133):

> God, King, in your omnipotence,
> Let my craft and my common sense
> Not be lost to me out of fear
> When before the king I must appear
> To answer Ysengrin in court.

No one in the *Roman* is wholly admirable. Every character will use his powers unjustly—even the weakest, like Coward the hare—when he gets a chance. Bricemer the stag, an animal of particular fair-mindedness, is constantly making important errors in judgment which the others, respecting his opinion, do not perceive. (One is reminded here of Charlemagne's most respected source of counsel, Duke Naimon, whose wisdom always provided poor advice.) The vanity of totally innocent creatures like Chanteclere increases their vulnerability, and Dame Pinte's prudence becomes a source of ostentatious self-esteem. Renard's independence thus comes to seem a proof of superior values, while the ineffectual brutes and weak-minded victims around him make us cherish the spirited sinner who takes them for his prey.

Pierre de Saint-Cloud, however, chose to give Renard an opponent superior to the wolf in *Ysengrimus*. Renard and Ysengrin are both described in the beginning of the poem as "mighty lords" and essentially equals. In Branch Va it is mentioned, quite arbitrarily, that Ysengrin speaks "several languages." We hear him, of course, only in French, and if his eloquence is not a match for Renard's, he is an effective speaker, not without finesse. He begins when addressing the court, for example, by emphasizing that Renard has not simply insulted Ysengrin but has broken the law. This is even more disrespectful to the king than to the husband and wife. Except for losing his way so that Hersent arrives at Maupertuis before him, Ysengrin does not show stupidity as much as he finds himself in a ridiculous position. He cannot accuse Renard without admitting that he witnessed the rape of his own wife and could do nothing about it. On the other hand, his attempts at guile do not go beyond seeking out the proposed judge Roenel, and it is the dog who contrives the crude plan of turning the oath taking into a murder. (One wonders how the other animals were supposed to have reacted to that event. Possibly it was hoped they would consider that a miracle had been accomplished by the dead "saint"!)

There are references, particularly in Branch I, to various occasions on which Renard made a fool of Ysengrin—getting him trapped in a pit, in a rich man's larder, in a frozen pond, in a monastery—but the cause of the war between them was more Renard's malice than Ysengrin's dull wits, and the fox escapes the wolf's immediate vengeance by speed rather than by cleverness.

Although Ysengrin is endlessly the victim of Renard, he never manages to inspire our sympathy. The fact that Hersent welcomes Renard in the first place does not increase our esteem for her husband, and his violence makes her seem, if not justified, at least courageous. He is gullible not, like King Mark, because he loves his wife, but entirely because of pride. Only the blind rage that overcomes him at the thought of a cuckold's horns makes it possible for him to appear in court at all, and this, too, makes him seem less than pitiable.

After Ysengrin, it is Bruin the bear who hates Renard the most, and his reasons are at least as good. He is neither cowardly nor excessively virtuous, but he does not seek personal vengeance, possibly because he lacks imagination. He will fight very effectively when forced to it but is otherwise not aggressive. It is he who protests when Noble wants to dismiss Ysengrin's case as unworthy of notice, but he seeks a legal rather than a martial solution. Nor does he make a formal complaint on his own behalf, but he does give, without embarrassment, a lengthy account of Renard's misdeeds to demonstrate the need for the court's intervention. On the other hand, when the council meets in Branch Va, the stag and the boar are far more scrupulous than Bruin is about the niceties of evidence.

Unlike the smaller and more intelligent Tibert the cat, Bruin does not hesitate to visit Maupertuis on the king's errand; in fact, he volunteers. Perhaps the false confidence given him by his size makes him unable to learn from experience. The love of honey that caused the extreme physical suffering he describes to the council has even more painful results in Branch I; the king, when Bruin falls fainting at his feet, thinks the bear is dead. When Renard makes his subsequent confession to Grinbert, however, he does not think the episode worthy of mention.

The name given to the king of all these beasts is not meant to be taken ironically. Noble may have his limitations, but he is not wholly unworthy as a monarch. He enjoys the respect of his subjects, including Renard who, after the trial, takes leave of Noble and the queen with a formality he shows no other members of the court. The ability to bring the accused and powerful baron to trial depends to some extent on the mystique of kingship. Grinbert will have no influence over Renard, safe in Maupertuis, unless he carries a letter sealed by the king.

Bruin, a blunt speaker, articulates the relation between the universal truce and the processes of law: if the king will not bring Renard to trial, Ysengrin cannot be expected to continue restraining himself. The king, however, would prefer another solution. He, like the rest of us, has a weakness for Renard, whose intelligence, he thinks, might well make an end of the wolf; and while Ysengrin's complaint is obviously justified, Noble is not inclined to regard it as a very serious matter. He offers Ysengrin fraternal consolation (Branch I, lines 49–50):

> And nowadays one sees all sorts
> Of cuckolds, even ruling courts!

He appeals to Ysengrin's sense of personal dignity and finally insists that Hersent be allowed her trial by ordeal, knowing that for Ysengrin the point is not Hersent's innocence—unlikely to be proved even if she carries a red-hot iron—but Renard's guilt. The king would prefer to avoid a direct confrontation that would mean either punishing a favorite or insulting a powerful vassal.

While King Noble's council has been much concerned with distinguishing admissible from inadmissible evidence, their master, finally enraged when he is shown the body of the murdered hen, requires nothing more to pronounce a verdict of guilty. Strictly speaking, Noble's first reaction is to have Renard summoned to court, but when Renard mistreats Bruin, the second summons is also a condemnation: Renard will be hanged. The lion will listen to nothing from the defense, and although he still goes through the form of asking his vassals for their advice, any who might have been inclined to debate the verdict are certainly much too terrified to speak. The lion rules because he is the strongest. Ultimately his whim is the only law.

Female characters in the *Roman* function as they probably did in the lives of most feudal lords: the women produce and care for the young, provide first aid, food, and comfort when their husbands come home, and play only secondary roles if they appear in public. Hersent is specifically assumed to be willing to say in court whatever her husband requires. This may be true, but she is also quite capable of deceiving Ysengrin. Hermeline's role in these early branches is practically negligible. She shows none of her husband's temperament, nor does she comment on his misadventures except to sympathize. She does not appear at all in "Renard's Pilgrimage." Renard seems to be alone in his lair to regret the passing years.

The most impressive female role belongs to Pinte the hen. She, like Hersent, is cleverer than her spouse, who seeks her advice but then refuses to take it. The plan to visit King Noble must have been hers, and it is her eloquence that dominates the scene at court, while Chanteclere merely weeps. Pinte has, moreover, the reputation of being a producer of extra-large eggs. It is interesting that Chaucer, far from crediting Chanteclere's wife with any such positive qualities, transforms her into a belittling purveyor of bad advice. Although Chaucer's cock's dream shows a fox more clearly than does the French version, Chaucer has the hen insist that the redness of the beast is due to an excess of bile in the dreamer's blood and that the proper response is not to stay at home in safety but to take a purgative. So, although he is splendidly erudite in opposing his wife's interpretation, the English Chanteclere puts himself in peril, while the author cheerfully comments on the coldness of women's counsel.

The conclusions about women that would be drawn from the *Roman de Renard* are standard medieval dogma: women's sexual appetite is greater than that of men, they have more brains and fewer scruples. Perhaps this is why Hermeline has so little to contribute: Renard plays both her part and his own.

The human characters who occasionally appear in these poems are not seen at Mass or at prayer but working on their farms or emerging from their houses, like the woman who lost the ripening cheese to the crow. However legitimate their fury against the creature who has stolen their possessions, they inspire little sympathy. Chanteclere, for all his vanity, is vastly more attractive as a spouse than the farmer Constant who screams curses at his wife before trying to rescue the cock. The humans, always more violent than the animals, are assisted by their dogs, who have a strangely intermediary role as both allies of men and, in the persona of Roenel, members of Noble's court. Perhaps that is why Roenel's reputation for probity is so ill deserved. The animal, pushed to the limit, snared or hunted by humans, always escapes. Aristocrats will not be defeated by peasants.

The success of the work depends on the delicate balance of human and animal attributes. Branch II begins with talk of a war between two great lords, but its early episodes concern barnyard animals threatened by a real fox, that is, a *goupil*. Only gradually do the characters emerge as members of a feudal society in which a hen's lamentations for her dead lord recall the lamentations of epic heroines, the fox and the wolf's wife engage in courtly, if rather hurried, conversation, and finally Ysengrin and Hersent emerge from the woods as noble vassals seeking redress from the king against one of their peers.

From this point on, the human aspects dominate, with the underlying world of real animals emerging just enough to provide an ironic counterpoint. Maupertuis is simultaneously a fortress and a fox's den: Bruin stops just outside the "barbican" because he is too large to get through the entrance. Grinbert nervously passes through courtyards and corridors but makes his entrance rear-end-first through a tunnel. The greater lords are mounted, including Tibert the cat who has to ride sidesaddle, but rarely is there a particular mention of the horses themselves.

The reader comes to think of the characters as individuals, more or less forgetting their physical appearance, until Ysengrin sits down with his tail between his legs, or the fur rises on the back of Hersent's neck. Sometimes an almost insignificant detail evokes the animal: Lord Bricemer walks "with his head held high" because of his antlers; Bernard the donkey swears by his hope of tender thistles; Renard, talking to the sheep, slips the word "grass" into his list of what worthy Christians are expected to sacrifice for God.

The reality of animal life *per se* is most apparent in the work of Pierre de Saint-Cloud. It is almost startling to find Lord Ysengrin hunting, nose to the ground; and Tibert, his whiskers gleaming with health, has visible teeth and claws to fight with, rather than knightly weapons. The author of "Renard's Pilgrimage" introduces the relationship between domestic beasts and their inconsiderate masters. The most intricate effects occur in "The Trial of Renard" where we encounter, with such delightfully mixed emotions, the grieving hens.

The octosyllabic couplets of the *Roman de Renart* are the "prose" of twelfth century vernacular fiction. The particular pleasure of reading or listening to rhymed narrative verse is in encountering a language apparently natural but unexpectedly musical. The very monotony of the meter has an incantatory effect. The rhyming sounds give an impression of inevitability to the events of the story and a childlike pleasure to the ear. The technical ease characteristic of these early branches confirms C. S. Lewis' description of the best medieval narrative style: "The story seems to be telling itself."[9]

It is possible to distinguish the verse of one poet from another on the basis of language alone, but only in the sense in which one potter's skill with the wheel might be compared to another's. Any critical comments are more likely to refer to the basic handling of the medium than to embellishment. There is great variety of tone and rhythm in all the branches, but a more smoothly worked complexity of sentence structure is apparent in Branch I.

The texture of Branches II and Va is distinctly rougher, that of Branch VIII plainer.[10]

It is from Branch I that one tends to select examples of the vigorous imagery that is part of the very substance of Old French, whose particularly forceful verbs may be difficult to approximate in either English or modern French: *coloier* describes Renard's craning his neck to look at forbidden hens; *ploier un cosin* occurs when Renard presses Grinbert against a comfortable pillow. *Jeta avant ses denz*, which describes the furious Tibert defending himself, means something between "leading with his teeth," which is too passive, and "hurling his teeth ahead of him." Comparing his teeth to grappling hooks, as in the translation, is more accurate, but the action no longer comes primarily from the verb. These authors do not strive for an originality of expression, which might detract from the story. To quote C. S. Lewis again, "the telling is for the sake of the tale."

Apart from these elusive Old French verbs—to which might be added *entr'oublier* (meaning "to forget," but not wholly) and a variety of wonderfully efficient expressions like *soi cinquieme* ("oneself and four others")—it is in some ways less difficult to translate Old French into English than to translate Old French into modern French. The medieval language is more strongly accented, its consonants are firmly pronounced, and there is no nasalization. Medieval octosyllabic verse corresponds very closely to iambic tetrameter. Nevertheless, the Germanic vigor of Old French is not to be matched even by English. Words like *ja* cannot be approached by "indeed" and must be built into the sentence in which they occur (similarly, *ainz*, a very emphatic "but"; *ez voz*, somewhere between "behold" and "here comes"; and *mar*, which indicates that something happened, was even fated to happen, to unfortunate effect).

The story, and the way in which it is told, however, can be brought into English essentially unchanged. Practically never will a literal translation offer a rhyme, but although the route may be somewhat different, it is possible to follow the events of the story and arrive at the same destination in nearly the same length of time. I have tried to stay close to the text in all details, and departures of any consequence are indicated in the notes.

CAST OF CHARACTERS

Bald, the rat (Pelez).
Baucent, the boar.
Belin, the sheep.
Bernard, the donkey, a high
  priest.
Bricemer, the stag, sene-
  schal to King Noble.
Bruin, the bear.
Chanteclere, the cock.
Clamor, the bull (Bruianz).
Cointereau, the monkey.
Constant de Noens, a
  wealthy farmer.
Copee, the murdered hen,
  sister of Pinte.
Coward, the hare.
Ferran, the packhorse.
Fiere, the lioness, wife to
  King Noble.
Frobert, the cricket.
Grinbert, the badger.
Hermeline, wife to Renard.
Hersent, wife to Ysengrin.
Lady Moire, the woodchuck.
Lanfroi, a forester.
Little Sticket, the ferret
  (Petit Porchaz).
Low, the mole.
Malebranche, son of Renard.

Martin de la Tour (Martin
  d'Orliens), son of the vil-
  lage priest.
Musard, a camel, presumably
  the jurist from Lombardy.
Noble, the lion, emperor and
  king of the beasts.
Petipas, the peacock.
Pinsard, son of Hersent.
Pinte, the hen, wife to
  Chanteclere.
Plateaux, the deer.
Renard, the fox.
Roenel, Frobert La Fontaine's
  watchdog.
Rovel, son of Renard.
Rusty, the squirrel, also
  known as Lord Roxat.
Shady (Percehaie), eldest son
  of Renard.
Short, the bitch (Corte).
Sir Gallopin, the hare.
Slow, the snail (Tardis).
Spiky, the hedgehog
  (Espinarz).
Spy, the skunk (Foinez).
Tibert, the cat.
Tiecelin, the crow.
Titmouse.
Ysengrin, the wolf.

Renard and Ysengrin the Wolf

My lords, you would hear nothing new*
If I proposed to offer you,
As other story-tellers have done,
A recital of how Paris won
Helen, and paid for his deceit.
After La Chievre* why repeat
Once more the tale of Tristan's woe?
Epic and comic rhymes you know
From the beginning to the end,
Of Yvain,* who was a lion's friend,
You all have heard, but never before
Has anyone described the war
That Ysengrin and his foe Renard
Fought so long and so very hard,
Determined to win at any cost.
The truth is, there was no love lost
Between these two at any time.
They thought that warfare was no crime,
And often enough the mighty lords*
Had faced each other and crossed swords.
Now hear the story—I'll include
Whatever is known to have caused their feud.*
   One day it happened that Renard—
Let whoever meets him be on guard
For he delights in doing harm—
Found, in his wanderings, a farm.*

*Notes, indicated by an asterisk, follow the text.

The farm was deep inside a wood.
Clearly the farmer's luck was good,*
For his lordship Constant de Noens,
30 Had a barnyard full of cocks and hens,
Donkeys and mallard ducks and geese.
In his house, close by, he lived in peace,
Wanting nothing for his pleasure:
His storerooms held a mighty treasure—
Capons and chickens by the score,
Bacon and hams and many more
Delicious things for him to eat,
And he was also rich in wheat.
Inside was every comfort found,
40 And he had orchards all around
Whose trees were laden with fine cherries,*

And there were different kinds of berries,
Apples and other fruits in sight.
Renard thought it all for his delight.
Around the barnyard oak stakes made
A high and sharp-edged palisade
With densely planted hawthorn hedges
Clustered against its outer edges.
Sir Constant was sure it would protect
50 His hens. Renard went to inspect,
Head lowered to avoid exposure;
Quiet, he goes toward the enclosure.*
But Renard, so skillful for the hunt,
Finds the thorns very far from blunt,
And time and again he turns away.
He can't come closer to his prey

Whether he lies low or springs out—
But the hens he cannot live without.
So he just crouches on the ground,
60   Perplexed, and looking all around.
If he jumps down from a perch too high,
The hens will see him in the sky:
Under the thorny hedge they'll scatter—
However fast he is, no matter,
Every one will be under cover.
Hard as he tries, he can't discover
How he could manage to surprise
The hens right there before his eyes,
Pecking away as their bellies fill.
70   Not one moment can Renard keep still.
At a corner of the fence he spied
A broken stake, and slipped inside.
Just where the fence posts didn't match,
The farmer had a cabbage patch;
Renard rushed through it with a leap,
And let himself fall down in a heap,
Hoping he wouldn't be detected.
But the ever-watchful hens suspected
The presence of an enemy,
80   And all of them made haste to flee.
    The rooster, my lord Chanteclere,
Had gone through the fence to a pathway near
The woods to have a pleasant time
On a dunghill that he liked to climb.
Majestic, feathers down to his feet,
He confronted the hens in their retreat,
Arching his neck as he inquired
Why, in such haste, they had retired.
Dame Pinte, who was wonderfully wise,
90   And whose eggs were of enormous size—
She had her perch on the rooster's right—
Explained the reason for their flight.
She said, "We had an awful scare."
"But why? What did you think was there?"

"It was some kind of dreadful beast—
Dangerous, to say the least!"
The cock said, "That is quite absurd.
A more foolish tale I never heard.
You all could perfectly well have stayed—
100   There was no reason to be afraid."
"There was, I tell you! I'm not blind
And I certainly haven't lost my mind!
I saw it right there in front of me!"
"And what exactly did you see?"
"What? I saw the hedges shake
And the cabbage leaves in the garden quake
Where someone found a place to hide."
"Pinte," said the cock, "be satisfied
With my opinion—it makes no sense
110   To worry. Inside that sturdy fence
Neither fox nor skunk would ever dare
To come. This ridiculous affair
Is now quite at an end, I trust."
The cock went back to scratch in the dust,
Being completely unconcerned
About taking any risks. He spurned
All dogs and foxes. Chanteclere
Was absolutely free from fear. *
What was standing before his very eyes
120   He could not see, he was so wise!
So, in his confidence, he posed,
One eye open, one eye closed,
One foot bent, one straight, aloof,
Resting up on top of a roof.
     Chanteclere stayed there at his station,
Feeling no special inclination
To keep watch or sing: he was disposed
To slumber. And the rooster dozed;
Then he fell asleep and dreamed,
130   So that to Chanteclere it seemed—
You'll think I made this up, of course,
But I am faithful to my source,

And you can take it for a fact
That the cock thought he was being attacked,
Inside the barnyard, tightly shut,
By—he didn't know exactly what,
But something to be scared about.
It was holding a ruddy garment out,
And along its edges he saw white
140   Bones which soon were pressing tight
Against his back. Poor Chanteclere,
Awakening, was still in fear,
And wondering why a dreadful foe
Should disturb his tranquil slumber so.
It seemed to him, when he awoke,
That it was a most peculiar cloak—
He'd been made to wear it inside out,
And he still could feel it closing about
His neck—he thought he'd suffocate.
150   His anguish was so very great
It was almost more than he could master.
What made his heart beat even faster
Was that, underneath, the cloak was white
And it wasn't made to be put on right—
Where it should open for the head
His tail was coming out instead.
Because of the dreams he shakes with fear;
He thinks his end is coming near,
That he will meet a dreadful fate—
160   He really is in an awful state.
His sleepiness has gone away,
And Chanteclere begins to pray:
"Oh, Holy Ghost, help me to stay
Free and safe from my foes today!"
Then the cock goes with the utmost speed,
As if he were in greatest need
Of protection, very much afraid,
Straight to the thorny palisade
With the hens all clustered underneath.
170   He calls to Pinte, having much belief

In her wisdom, takes her to one side,
And says, "From you I will not hide
My sorrow and my great dismay.
I think I'm marked out as the prey
Of some bird or beast, and all of you
May well become his victims too!"
Pinte said, "Oh, my lord, take care
What you say! It really isn't fair.
There's nothing at all for us to fear.
180   Listen to me! Come over here!
I swear by the saints we ask for help
You're like a little dog who'll yelp
While the stone is still high up in the air.
Whatever did you see out there
That you carry on about it so?"
"Pinte," says the cock, "what you don't know
Is that I was asleep, beyond the wall,
And I had a dream you'd have to call
A nightmare. When I've told my tale
190   You will understand why I'm so pale.
You shall hear every part of it—
Not one single thing will I omit—
Then I hope you'll tell me what to do.
I dreamed that I saw coming through
The barnyard, filling me with dread,
Some beast whose fur-lined cloak was red—
No shears were used when it was made—
And then I felt it being laid
Upon my back—I couldn't fight.
200   Along its edges there were white
Little bones that were very strong;
The collar had been put on wrong,
And it was certainly too small,
It hurt me so. The fur was all
Turned to the outside. I went in
By the neckhole, struggling hard to win
My freedom, and, before long, somehow
I got out backwards. Even now

I can see that dreadful creature's tail
210 Where its head should be, and I still quail.
Pinte, now that you've heard me speak
I'm sure that you won't think I'm weak
Because my heart is quaking so.
But now what I would like to know
Is the meaning of this visitation.
Tell me, what's your interpretation?
By the faith you swore me, on your oath."
Pinte replied—she was nothing loath—
"I swear, for the way you told your dream
220 I haven't very much esteem—
In fact it's nothing but a lie,
And I'll be glad to tell you why.
      The strange creature who appeared
In your dream, that you so greatly feared,
The unknown beast of whom you spoke
Who wore a red and fur-lined cloak,
That is the fox—as soon as you
Told of its ruddy fur I knew.
The garment you were forced to wear
230 Which caused you such anguish and despair
Was edged with what you thought was bone
But was really teeth! This is shown
By the collar that you found so tight
And said had not been put on right—
That's how the creature will be fed
When his mouth clamps shut around your head!
That is indeed the way you'll wear
The garment, if you don't take care!
As for the waving tail you thought
240 Was upside down, when you are caught
You'll be hanging from the fox's jaws
And see his tail between his paws.
I swear to you, by the faith I hold,
You won't be saved by silver or gold;
Your life will be lost, I have no doubt.
As for the cloak that seemed inside out,

The fox in thick warm fur is clad
Which stands on end when the weather's bad.
Now you know—every word I said is true—
250   What your dream was really telling you,
And it will happen just that way
Before noontime this very day
Unless you make up your mind to hide.
Come back with me—we'll stay inside. *
Believe me, you really must beware,
For the fox is hiding right out there
In that bush, and he will have a scheme
To capture you, as in your dream."
    When the cock had heard Pinte explicate
260   His vision, he was most irate.
"What's clear, Pinte, is you're out of your mind!
And you are anything but kind
When you say some beast is in the yard
Who will not find it very hard
To strike me down with a mortal blow.
A curse on whoever scorns me so!
Nothing you've said gives me concern.
I don't think I have much to learn
Of dreams from you; it cannot be
270   That I'll come to grief as you foresee."
"My lord, God grant that it be so.
But if I'm wrong in what I know
I grant you permission, on my life,
No longer to have me as your wife!"
"There's no truth, Pinte, in what you said."
He put her warnings out of his head,
And, far from doing what she asked,
Went back to the dunghill where he basked
In the sun, and soon began to doze. *
280   When Renard, who has been watching, knows
Chanteclere's asleep (he takes no chances,
Prudent Renard), then he advances.
Renard, who's a master of such ruses
He can cheat anyone he chooses,

Will not delay a moment more.
Putting one silent foot before
The other—you would not have known
That he was made of flesh and bone—
He holds his head down, stays under cover,
290   Hoping Chanteclere won't discover
How close he is to being caught,
So that patience won't have been for naught.
    When Renard had come quite close to his prey,
He made a grab for him right away,
But in his eagerness he missed,
And Chanteclere, with a jumping twist—
He had recognized Renard on sight—
To the top of the dunghill fled in fright.
For Renard it was a dreadful shock
300   To realize he'd lost the cock.
Raging, he tried to find a way
Still to seize that delicious prey
He had waited for the whole day long.
Renard said, "Chanteclere, you are wrong
To greet my arrival with alarm.
I would not do you any harm
For you're practically my closest kin."*
Chanteclere's trust wasn't hard to win,
And in his joy he began to crow.*
310   Renard said, "Cousin, your singing so
Makes me remember Chanteclin
Your late lamented sire—he'd begin
Crowing his best, and the great scope
Of his voice left no one else a hope
Of matching him; for miles around
The entire world could hear that sound!
At certain moments his eyes would close
And he'd outsing anyone he chose!"
"I think that if you praise my kin,
320   It's because you hope to do me in!"
"No, good cousin, you do me wrong.
Close your eyes, let me hear a song!

In your veins and mine the same blood flows;
I would rather lose a foot, God knows,
Than have you hurt. To strike a blow
At a relative! Who'd stoop so low?"
"I cannot believe in your good will,
But if you'll stand away from this hill,
The neighbors will not have any choice
330 But to hear the brilliance of my voice
And the great beauty of my song."
"Sing, cousin! Show me that you belong
To the lineage of Chanteclin!"
So spoke Renard with a little grin
That he was careful not to show.
Chanteclere begins to crow,
But afraid Renard had told him lies,
He closes only one of his eyes
And while he sings remains on guard,
340 Looking around to watch Renard
Who says, "If you have sung your best,
I must tell you that you failed the test.
With his eyes closed, Chanteclin was stronger,
He could hold his notes much longer—
On twenty farms his song was heard."
Chanteclere, believing every word,
Sings again, and with all his might,
Lets himself go, with his eyes shut tight.
At that Renard, in the cabbage patch,
350 Waits not an instant more to snatch
His victim by the throat and run,
Joyful because at last he'd won.
Pinte, watching Renard leave*
With Chanteclere, can only grieve.
Feeling utterly forlorn
She eloquently starts to mourn,
Saying, "I told you so, my lord,
But mockery was my reward—
You thought that I was out of my mind!
360 Now, captured by Renard, you find

How true was every word I spoke
That you, in your wisdom, thought a joke.
But I was a fool because I taught
A fool—always fearless till he's caught.
And now, alas, Renard has fled,
And I might just as well be dead;
I have lost my lord, and there can be
No honor left in this world for me!"*
    The housewife opened the garden gate.
370 She had seen that it was getting late—
Time for vespers—but, call as she might,
The hens weren't coming in for the night.
She shouted, "Pinte! Bise! Rosette!"
But not one answer did she get,
And she began to be afraid
That somehow the chickens might have strayed.
And then she gave a mighty shout
For the cock Renard was dragging out!
She tried, in her fury, to give chase,
380 But he saw her and increased his pace.
There was no way, however hard she tried,
To catch him. "Help! Help!" she cried.
Some peasants playing a game nearby
Came running up to find out why,
Loudly clamoring for her to tell
What it was that had made her yell.
"Alas," she says between her sighs,
"I have just seen with my own eyes
A dreadful thing, and I greatly fear—"
390 "What?" "That I've lost poor Chanteclere!
The fox took him—he'll be seen no more."
Constant said, "You ugly whore!
How could you let him get away?"
"How could I help it?" "Make him stay!"
"I swear by the saints above I tried!"
"By God, then you should have had his hide!
Couldn't you hit him?" "With what, pray tell?"
"With this stick right here!" "But he ran too well,

And he gave such mighty leaps and bounds—
400 He could outrace two Breton hounds."
"Where'd he go?" "That way! Straight ahead!"
And the whole band of peasants sped
After the fox, shouting, "Here! Over here!"
Renard, as they were drawing near,
Went leaping into a hole he found
And hit his rear end on the ground
So hard they heard him when he landed.
Constant, in the lead, commanded:
"Now's our chance! Hurry up! We've won!"
410 And even faster the peasants run.
Constant calls his dog, and the rest
Summon fierce Daggertooth and Highcrest,
Bardol, Malvoisin,* Hammerhead,
And set them after Renard the Red!*
So men and hunting dogs give chase
And soon enough they find the place
Where Renard is hiding. "He's in here!"
They shout. It's all up with Chanteclere
Unless he thinks up a plan right now:
420 "I'm surprised, my lord, that you allow
This shameful treatment. I expected
That you would make yourself respected,
But here is Constant close on your heels
Shouting insults as if he feels
You've met your master. Why not wait
Close to the door and set him straight?
Then you'll be well placed to mock
The peasants who cry, 'He's got the cock!' "
    Even the wisest, once in a while,
430 Are fooled. Renard whose craft and guile
Give him in all the world no peer
Was taken in by Chanteclere.
As he shouted to them in his pride,
"Your rooster's mine!" his mouth opened wide,
And Chanteclere, when he felt the jaws
Unclench, did not for an instant pause

But flapped his wings, flew up and clung
To an apple tree. On a pile of dung.
Renard, down below, was pensive, sad,
440   Furious to think that he'd been had.
Then the rejoicing Chanteclere
Laughed at him, and said, with a jeer,
"Isn't that just the way it goes!
In this world we have many woes."
To which Renard, embittered, said,
"May he, for shame, never raise his head
Who has so little wit and skill,
He babbles when he should keep still."
"So be it," Chanteclere replies,
450   "And may that fool lose both his eyes
Who has so little wit he'll take
A nap when he should stay awake.
After what you have done today,
Who will believe a word you say?
How wonderful to be your kin—
It very nearly did me in!
Crooked Renard, I recommend
You bring your visit to an end,
For if you linger you may find
460   You have to leave your skin behind."
Renard has no desire to hear
Another word from Chanteclere,
Nor has he any wish to speak.
He turns away and runs, so weak

38

From hunger his heart can scarcely beat,
Grieving over his defeat,
And cursing all the time he's wasted,
Because the cock escaped untasted.
    Lamenting, through the woods he fled
470   Until he saw just above his head
A titmouse on a hollow oak
Where she had laid her eggs. He spoke
Courteously of the great delight
He felt at that appealing sight:
"Dear friend, what a joy to meet like this!*
Come down right now, I want a kiss!"
"Renard," the bird said, "that will do!
I would indeed be friends with you
If you weren't such a lying cheat!
480   Everyone knows what your deceit
Has cost the many beasts and birds
You've taken in with honeyed words.
What will become of you, I wonder.
Devils have dragged you so far under
No one is left who'll trust you now."
"Lady, by the baptismal vow
That made me godfather to your son,
I swear I've never said or done
Anything that could cause you harm.
490   And do you know why your alarm
Is now a foolishness indeed?
King Noble the lion has decreed
That there shall be peace in all his lands,
And every vassal he commands
Has sworn that he will do his part
So no new argument can start—
God willing, they will keep the truce.
So now you see why there's no use
In being afraid. At last the poor
500   Will have a chance to feel secure;
They're overjoyed—they need no longer
Fear lest the quarrels of the stronger

Bring them the suffering of war—
That will not happen anymore."
"Is that what you're hoping I'll believe?*
Better find someone more naive!
Nothing that you can find to say
Will win a kiss from me today."

    Seeing that one he holds so dear

510   Will not believe that he's sincere,
"Lady," the fox said, "you're unjust,
But I know how to win your trust!
I'll close my eyes and stand right here;
Then you can kiss me with no fear."
To that the titmouse said, "All right!
But be sure you keep your eyes closed tight!"
That's all it took; the titmouse dived,
Having no desire to kiss, contrived
To twist his whiskers and to toss

520   A handful* of dried leaves and moss
Right in his face—when he would have fed
On the bird, that's what he got instead.
The wily titmouse as she fled
Shouted, "What was that you said
About peace? There would have been no lack
Of bloodshed, had I not turned back.
I thought the king would not allow
Fighting, and you had made a vow
To keep the peace throughout the land.

530   I see how you honor his command!"
Renard laughed gaily as he spoke:
"But that was only a little joke
To give you, just for fun, a scare.
Come try again, and I'll play fair.
I'll keep my eyes closed tight like this,
And you can give me a friendly kiss."
"Very well," she answers, "we will try it,
If you promise me that you'll keep quiet!"
She flies down very close to his jaws,

540   Grazing them, but she does not pause.

That way she isn't caught in the trap
When Renard's teeth close with a wicked snap.
"Who would still wonder," says the bird,
"Whether or not to trust your word?
If I should believe the lies you tell,
Let the devil burn my soul in Hell!"
Renard says, "You're not brave enough!
I thought that you would call my bluff,
Knowing that I would never be
550 A traitor to my own family!
But one more time fly down to me—
Where there are two there must be three.
In the name of everything that's good,
I beg you to show you've understood
That I would never do you harm,
And that you were wrong to take alarm.
My lovely friend, come down once more!
I ask it by the faith you swore
To me and my godson that we see
560 Singing there on the linden tree.
There is forgiveness for sinners too!"
But nothing he could say or do
Would make her see truth in his pretense,
For she had much too much good sense
Not to stay in safety way up high.
All of a sudden they hear the cry
Of hunting dogs and the awful noise
Of galloping huntsmen, shouting boys,
And the shrill and mellow hunting horns,
570 A music that not the bravest scorns!
Renard doesn't even pause to check.
He knows they are breathing down his neck.
His tail is arched up over his back,
Anticipating the dogs' attack.
Hearing the hunting horns, who lags?
Renard has already packed his bags.
And the titmouse from above calls out,
"Is this the peace you told me about?

I thought you said that war was banned.
580   It's more than I can understand
Why you are leaving in such haste."
Renard doesn't have much time to waste,
But as he goes he lies once more:
"Lady, to keep the peace we swore
In all good faith, and we won't forget,
But some don't know about it yet—
The very ones who are coming now.
The vassals who were to take the vow
Assembled on the appointed day.
590   They solemnly promised to obey
The king's royal proclamation
And keep the peace throughout the nation,
But these could not even be allowed—
They are so young—to join the crowd."
"Renard, what you say is just not fair!
Why should you think they aren't aware
That we're all at peace? Don't run away!
Where's my kiss?" "I haven't time today,
But your own lord—I was there and heard—
600   Has taken the oath and will keep his word."
Renard, knowing all the shortcuts, flees.
Suddenly, on the path, he sees
A holy man* accompanied
By two big dogs on a heavy lead.
Behind him Renard could hear the hunt

Getting closer, and the boy in front,
Seeing the dogs who don't look slow,
Cried to the friar, "Let them go!
Look! There's the fox! He's going by!"
610   Renard heard that, and gave a sigh.
It will go hard with him, he knows,
If he should be captured by his foes—
Once they have him, he'll lose his life.
Each huntsman carries a sharp-pointed knife
That could rip the fur right off his back—
And ferocity isn't what they lack!
He shudders to think he'll lose his skin
Unless intelligence can win
Over their strength, and he has never
620   Felt such a need for being clever.
The friar stands considering,
And Renard, who can't do anything,
Neither go forward nor retreat,
Nor find a way to avoid defeat,
Feels that he's trapped as in a box.
And then the friar sees the fox.
"Ha, ha! you vermin, here you are!
And I don't think you'll be going far!"
"Reverend Sir, for God's sweet sake,
630   I beg you not to make a mistake!
Surely it would never do
For a hermit, a saintly man like you
To be guilty of a dreadful wrong.
If I should be detained here long
By you or by your dogs, you'd commit
A sin, and I would grieve for it.
The loss to me would be your disgrace.
What you see here is only a race
To see if those dogs can beat my speed,
640   And the winner's purse is fat indeed."
    This tale the friar swallows whole,
And so, commending the fox's soul

To Saint Julian and to the Lord,
He goes his way. Renard can't afford
To linger there; he sets his course
Along the valley, spurring his horse,
And gallops hard across a field.
But those behind him do not yield—
They were gaining on him very fast
650   When Renard got rid of them at last;
Over a mighty ditch he went,
And the dogs completely lost his scent.
Renard was not in the least inclined
To wait; he left them far behind
Having, to say the least, good cause
To fear their mighty teeth and jaws.
No wonder that he felt so tired!
To escape his enemies required
All his strength, so many miles he'd fled,
660   But who cares? At least he wasn't dead.
Now finally he is on his way.
But the misadventures of the day
Have been painful for him, and he goes
Cursing and threatening his foes.
    Grumbling bitterly in his wrath,
Renard encountered in his path
Tibert the cat, who was all alone,
But having lots of fun on his own.
Whirling, twisting himself around*
670   His tail, he made a mighty bound
And then another from whose height
All of a sudden he caught sight
Of Renard, who watched and did not stir.
Tibert knew him by his ruddy fur.
The cat was all ready to engage
In pleasantries. Renard, in a rage,
Said, "Tibert, I think that you should know
My greeting to you would be a blow—
And if you get close enough I'll try it."
680   Tibert was keeping very quiet.

Seeing the fox in such a mood
The cat, neither cowardly nor rude,
Approached Renard and spoke with poise:
"If something I have done annoys
Your lordship, that's much to my regret."
Renard's long fast wasn't broken yet,
And he'd run too far—he could not seek
A quarrel, he was much too weak—
He hadn't eaten all day long.
690   While Tibert, rested and very strong,
Had whiskers that were gleaming white,
Teeth that were clearly made to bite,
And claws that could pierce the toughest skin.
I think if Renard should try to win
He would meet an adequate defense,
But the hungry fox has too much sense;
(Many a lengthy scar he bore
From battles they had fought before.)
So now he speaks in a different tone:
700   "Tibert," he says, "I want it known
That I'm at war—war to the end—
With a kinsman who was once my friend,*
With Ysengrin. I have in my hire
Many good soldiers, but my desire
Is for you to join them and take my side.
Never will I be satisfied
Until I have brought him to his knees."
And Tibert joyfully agrees.
Not for an instant does he pause
710   Before taking up the fox's cause;
Looking at him most earnestly,
He says, "Sir Renard, you can count on me!
You'll never find my valor lacking,
And all the more since we're attacking
Lord Ysengrin. I have a great need
To pay him back for word and deed."
And so the two of them agreed
On the services each guaranteed,

And went on together as allies.
720 To believe Renard is most unwise.
All he wants is to betray
Tibert, and soon he'll find a way.
His hatred has only been concealed.
And then a narrow path revealed
A likely chance. Some distance ahead,
Close to the woods, the road led
To where a hidden trap had been laid
By a peasant. It was strongly made
From the split branches of an oak—
730 To get caught in there would be no joke.
Renard has little love for Tibert:
If he is trapped, he'll be badly hurt.
And Renard says with a friendly smile,
"Tibert, I so admire your style—
Your good looks, valor, and, of course,
The wonderful swiftness of your horse.
Give me a sample, if you would;
It's sandy here, the footing's good,
And it would be, I think, great fun
740 To see how he can really run—
The path is straight and smooth and level."
Renard's an offspring of the devil,
Trying to lead the cat to woe,
And Tibert's all too ready to go.
Bounding along with a mighty stride,
Suddenly, by good luck, he spied
The trap, and knew the fox intended
To do him mischief. Tibert pretended
Still that everything was fine,
750 And moved a little out of his line,
Just enough so he wasn't trapped.
Renard, not failing to see it, snapped,
"No one could say your run was great—
Your horse wasn't even going straight!"
Tibert wasn't quite as close as before.
"Come on!" said Renard. "Let's try once more.

There's no way you can win a race,
If you're wandering all over the place!"
"What makes you say that?" "I observed
760 That the path was straight, but your horse swerved."
    And Tibert began to run flat out,
But not at all forgetting about
The trap. He made a very high
Jump, and of course Renard knew why.
Tibert had clearly understood,
So the fox's plan would be no good.
He looks for the proper words to say
That will trick the cat another way,
Comes up to Tibert with enough control
770 To conceal the evil in his soul,
And says, "Tibert, allow me to tell you why
No one with any sense would buy
That horse of yours. The way he shies
And jumps around, he would be no prize."
Tibert took up his mount's defense:
Sir Renard's objection made no sense,
And Tibert kept racing to and fro,
Faster all the time, to show
That the fox was wrong to criticize.
780 Then they had a nasty surprise:
Two big watchdogs running hard
Began to bark when they saw Renard.
Tibert and the fox took off in fear
(One running, one kicking from the rear)
Until they came in their headlong race
To where the trap had been set in place.
Renard saw it, would have turned aside,
But Tibert, pressing him stride for stride,
Gave him a shove, his foot fell in
790 And so dislodged the central pin.
The little doors that were open wide
Snapped shut with the fox's foot inside.
So well was the mechanism made,
That where he landed, there he stayed.

Tibert gave Renard his due respect
When he struck at him to such effect
That he'd very soon be made to pay
For his misdeeds in a painful way—
Never did Sir Renard intend
800   To keep faith with his ally and friend.
And Tibert, even in full flight,
Shouts at the fox with all his might:
"Renard, Renard, you'll stay right there
While I go my way as free as air.
My lord, I wasn't born yesterday,*
And turnabout is just fair play.
There's not much chance for fancy dodging
When this is what you have for lodging!"
No doubt Renard's in serious trouble:
810   The peasant's coming on the double,
He's fighting off the dog's attacks,
And now the man has raised his axe—
The fox would have parted with his head,
But the blow fell on the oak instead,
And the piece that held his foot was split
While he himself wasn't even hit.
He only felt an awful jolt;
His foot was hurting, but he could bolt,
Unhappy about his injury
820   But glad enough that he was free
And hadn't left his foot behind.
When the trap broke he was not inclined

To think up a complicated plan,
But simply picked himself up and ran.
The peasant hollers, raging mad
Because he knows that he's been had;
The dogs accelerate their pace
Barking and yapping as they race.
And until he has left the woods behind
830   Renard doesn't even try to find
A hiding place. The two dogs, tired,
Turn back, but Renard goes on inspired
By fear, although he is in great pain.
He gallops down an endless lane
With no idea where he should go.
He feels desperate, but even so
Thinks how quickly a leg can snap
When caught in such a terrible trap.
It will have to be a long time yet
840   Before he can manage to forget
The peasant's terrifying axe.
And so, not daring to relax,
He goes his way as fortune wills.*

     At last, in a plain between two hills,
He came upon a lovely site.
There was a river on the right,
Just at the edge of a mountain's slope,
And it looked so peaceful he could hope
He might in that place be out of reach.
850   He crossed the river to a beech
That was planted there, circled around,
Keeping his nose close to the ground,
Then lay on the cool grass, rolling about,
Taking his ease and stretching out.
The lodgings truly were ideal—
Provided he could find a meal,
He would be very glad to stay.
Another who'd fasted long that day
Was my lord Tiecelin the crow.
860   Now hunger forces him to go

Out of the woods and through the skies
Until, far down below, he spies
What seems a likely looking farm
And, careful that no one take alarm,
Flies close and to his pleasure sees
A thousand pieces of good cheese
Set out to ripen in the sun.*
And just then there wasn't anyone
On guard lest man or beast decide
870 To help himself—she'd gone inside,*
The one who'd been assigned the task,
And Tiecelin didn't have to ask
Whether his moment had arrived,
But instantly took aim and dived,
Grabbing the cheese. There was a shout
As the old woman came rushing out:
"You'll never get away with it!"
And she tried with pebbles and stones to hit
The crow—she had just about gone crazy.
880 He said, "Is it my fault if you're lazy?
Whether you call it wrong or right
The cheese was out there in plain sight—
I only had to open my claws:
Bad shepherds help the wild wolf's cause.
This cheese is mine, so do your best
To make sure nobody gets the rest.
I took the risk, for the cheese appeared
Just right to lather up my beard,*
Tender and of a yellow hue;
890 The way it smelled it would taste good too.
Now, thanks to you, I shall retire
To my nest and make a cooking fire
So I can boil and roast my cheese*
And then enjoy it at my ease."
    With that Tiecelin withdrew,
And pausing not at all he flew
To where Renard would meet the crow,
The one above and the other below,

With equal justice on each side*
900   Except that the fox's belly cried
For food, and the other had a feast.
The cheese wasn't hardened in the least,
And Tiecelin, with all his might,
Was pecking away to get a bite
Of the yellow creamy part inside.
To no avail had that women tried
To keep him from enjoying it!
He hammered away, and a little bit
He didn't notice fell to the ground
910   Close to Renard, who looked around,
And there was someone he thought he knew.
He shook his head—it couldn't be true!—
Got up for a better view, and saw,
With the cheese gripped tightly in his claw,
A kinsman and friend of long ago.
The fox called softly to the crow:
"In God's name, I can't believe my eyes!
This is such a wonderful surprise!
Dear friend, is it really you? I pray
920   That God in heaven will bless today
Your late lamented sire whose voice
So often made my heart rejoice.
Certainly it was not by chance
That Rohart won every prize in France!
And you yourself, I know, have sung
Beautifully when you were young—
I'd be most grateful if you would deign
To sing me some charming old refrain."*
The flattered beast croaks out a phrase
930   That Renard is very quick to praise:
"You have made great progress in technique,
But your high notes sound a little weak.
You'd only have to clear your throat,
To increase your range by at least one note."
Proud Tiecelin did not hesitate;
He cawed again. "By God, that's great!"

Cried Renard. "Your voice is so pure and clear,
If you gave up eating nuts* we'd hear
A song that would truly be sublime.
940   Do let me listen one more time!"
The crow uttered a mighty screech,
Trying to get his voice to reach
Still higher, but the claw that gripped
The cheese relaxed, the treasure slipped
And fell to the ground at Renard's feet.
But he, that master of deceit—
Woe to the one he takes for prey!—
Just simply left it where it lay
Hoping, by this joy deferred,
950   That he'd also get to eat the bird.
The cheese is in plain sight on the ground.
Renard gets up and staggers around;
One foot behind the other drags,
His skin hangs off him like tattered rags
(Even though he had finally managed
To flee the trap, his leg was damaged).
All this for Tiecelin's benefit.
"Alas," says Renard, "that God sees fit
To afflict me with such miseries!
960   By Saint Mary, I swear that cheese—
God's curse on it, it smells so strong—
Will do me in before too long!
For everyone I know agrees
There's nothing so bad for wounds as cheese.
It's strictly forbidden in my diet.
I haven't the least desire to try it.
I beg you, Tiecelin, come down here!
If you don't help, my end is near!
I wouldn't dream of troubling you,
970   But my leg was just about cut through
The other day when I had the mishap
Of getting caught in a peasant's trap.
I couldn't manage to keep out,
And now I should not be running about

But convalescing from that disaster
With my poor leg wrapped up in plaster."
  Tiecelin believes all that he hears,
Seeing his friend Renard in tears.
He comes down from his perch up high—
980 A great mistake and he'll soon know why.
If Renard should grab him and not let go,
There wouldn't be much left of the crow.
But Tiecelin doesn't come too near,
And Renard attempts to calm his fear:
"You have no reason for alarm.
Come here! Could a cripple do you harm?"
And Renard went closer to the crow,
Poor fool, who was flying much too low
And didn't know what was happening
990 Until the fox gave a mighty spring.
He missed. But Tiecelin did bequeath
Four feathers to Renard's sharp teeth.
The crow was frightened and dismayed
To find his friendship so betrayed.
He looked himself over front and back:
"I left myself open to attack,"
He said. "My God, how little sense
I had not to see through his pretense—
That treacherous, lying, foul red beast—
1000 And now he has pulled out at least
Four feathers from my right wing and tail—
May God make his health and powers fail!
Renard is a false friend and a liar—
I have all the proof that I require!"
  Renard explained that he meant no harm,
But Tiecelin found little charm
In listening to him; furious
He wasn't the least bit curious
To find out if his fright was justified.
1010 "Help yourself to the cheese," he cried,
"You can be sure that's all you'll get
From us today.* What I regret

Is that any fool should have understood
From your acting that you meant no good."
Renard didn't bother to insist;
He was making up for what he missed
By eating the cheese to the last bit,
But there wasn't very much of it:
The way it went down his throat you'd think
1020   It had been some kind of delicious drink!*
You could look in any land you please
And never would you find such cheese;
He had eaten cheese his whole life long
And certainly he could not be wrong.
Nor did his injured leg hurt more.
    So did Renard add up the score;
And having said all he had to say,
Made up his mind to go his way.
    Renard cut through the woods until,
1030   As he was going down a hill,
He turned as he had not intended
Through the dense underbrush that ended
Just at a hedge with a dark hollow
Underneath it. What would follow
Was something he'd be sorry for,
In fact it was what would cause the war,
By the devil's will and mortal sin,
With King Noble's marshal* Ysengrin.
Renard wasn't sure how he should behave
1040   When he came closer to the cave,
But wanting a place to rest and hide,
He was already deep inside
And standing in the vaulted hall*
When he realized that he'd come to call
On Lord Ysengrin, his bitter foe.
Four wolf cubs were lying there below,
Close to their mother, Madame Hersent,
All of them peaceful and content
As she nursed each one with tender care.
1050   They were newborns, but her head was bare.*

She was startled to see the sunlight pour
Into her den through the open door
Behind which the lithe Renard had hidden.
She looked to see who had come unbidden.
Hersent, who was feeling quite concerned,
Relaxed again as soon as she learned,
Recognizing the ruddy fur,
Just who was there to visit her.
She saw that Renard could not keep still,
1060   And said, with a laugh that showed good will,
"Renard, what are you looking for?"
He could have gone right through the floor
For shame, and could not speak for fear—
Ysengrin scarcely held him dear.
Hersent jumped up, her head held high,
Looking the fox straight in the eye
And pointing her finger at him said,
"Renard, Renard, your coat is as red
As you are sly and your manners vile.
1070   You've paid me no visit all this while,
So surely, after such neglect,
If you come here now you can't expect
To be called a kinsman or a friend."
Terror did its best to lend
Eloquence to Renard's reply:
"Lady, please let me tell you why
My congratulations are so late.
I feel for you anything but hate
And would have come sooner if I could,
1080   But whenever I'm in this neighborhood
I have to take the greatest care—
Lord Ysengrin is everywhere,
And all my hope is to avoid him
Because, in some way, I've annoyed him.
Yet truly your husband Ysengrin
In hating me commits a sin.
May my flesh endure a hundred pains
If I am guilty, as he complains,

Of loving you as I should not do!*
1090   Wherever he goes he says that's true,
Lying about me to his friends,
Letting them know that he intends
To pay them well if they succeed
In shaming me by some evil deed.
But tell me, doesn't such a claim
Also reflect on your good name?
I don't like to be falsely accused,
And had I spoken, you'd have refused."
Hersent, as she listened to him, burned
1100   With rage and shame at what she learned.
"My lord Renard, can it really be
That that's the way they speak of me?
I never suspected it, alas.
But sometimes, you know, it comes to pass
That defending honor prematurely
Means to defend it very poorly.
If I who have lived a blameless life
Can yet be called an unworthy wife,
It seems to me it is only fair
1110   To inaugurate that love affair
Right here and now. Let me have your heart;
You'll be my love, and for a start
Come here and kiss me! What better place?
No one can see how we embrace."
Renard, full of joy and jubilation,
Thanks Hersent for her invitation
With a pleasure he does not disguise
As she makes him room between her thighs.
But Renard thinks he had best not stay.
1120   Ysengrin won't be long away
And might at any moment appear—
What better cause could there be for fear?
But before he left he went and peed
On the wolf cubs, as had been agreed,*
And took whatever there was to eat,
Throwing out old and fresh-killed meat,

Dragged the cubs from their cozy bed,
Cursed them, hit them over the head
And called them filthy bastards, as cruel
1130   As if he were teaching them in school.
Who cares how anyone reacts?
With no one witnessing his acts
To be careful of except Hersent,
And she, it would seem, was quite content.
When he left, the wolf cubs all were crying,
And their mother came to see them, trying
To soothe and comfort them so well
That they would be willing not to tell.
"Children," she said, "by the faith you owe
1140   To me, your father must not know
That you ever saw Renard in here—
I ask it as you hold me dear."
"The devil you say! Do you expect
That we should be willing to protect
That foul traitor Renard the Red
When we'd all be glad if he were dead?
And you allowed him to come right in,
Wife as you are to Ysengrin.
Can we forget how we are treated?
1150   With God's help Renard shall be defeated!"
    Renard hears the bitter argument
The cubs were having with Hersent.
He hurries, slinking close to the ground
So he'll not so easily be found,
And takes up his journey once again.
Meanwhile, back at the wolf's deep den,
Hollowed out beneath the stone,
Lord Ysengrin returns alone.
He is happy to be home at last,
1160   Having run so many miles so fast,
Tracking down and capturing his prey
Until he had meat enough to weigh
Almost too much for his strong back.
Little does he care what others lack!

So he returns to his family
With which Renard had been making free,
And his sons rush up to tell their woes,
How they'd taken from Renard hard blows,
How he'd pissed on them, emptied their store,
1170   Called them bastard sons of a whore—
"And you yourself that traitor scorns,
Saying you should be wearing horns."
Ysengrin nearly lost his head
On hearing what his children said.
He almost fainted, then roared and screamed
Just like a raging devil he seemed:
"Hersent, what do you take me for?
You vile, stinking, lousy whore,
I've cherished you and held you dear,
1180   You've not known either want or fear
And you let someone else between your legs!
Who, in vain, for your favor begs
When Renard the Red, that louse, that twit,
That filthy, spineless, little shit
Mounted you just like a mare!
That's too much! By God's heart I swear
You have done such damage to my pride
You'll never again lie at my side,
If you ever dare to cross my will."*
1190   Hersent knew she'd have no life until
She gave him the answer he required:
She would do all that he desired.
"My lord," she said, "I deserve more trust.
I think you are terribly unjust.
You rage when it would make more sense
To let me prove my innocence.
I am quite willing to submit
To trial or ordeal as you see fit;
If that doesn't prove it's your mistake,
1200   Then have me hanged or burned at the stake.
But most of all I want you to know
There's nothing I wouldn't do to show

You have only to ask and I'll obey."
Ysengrin doesn't know what to say.
Now that he's listened to her speak
He feels his anger growing weak.
And finally he makes her give
Her promise that Renard won't live—
Let him beware!—another hour
1210 If ever again he's in her power.*

 Looking and feeling fine once more,
Ysengrin says he'll end the war
Before it gets started, and Renard
From now on had best be on his guard.
Then Ysengrin set out to seek
His foe, and it hadn't been a week
Before there was a strange event.*
When Renard had left the path he went*
To an orchard he found close at hand,
1220 Fenced in where they had cleared the land.
After they harvested a crop
Of peas, they let all the haulms drop
And now they had piled them to one side.
That made Renard a place to hide.
He had often travelled there, intent
On casting about to find a scent
That might provide him with a meal.
Ysengrin too thought the place ideal
When, nose to the ground, he became aware
1230 That Renard, the prey he sought, was there.
In his excitement he gave a shout.
Renard knew his voice, and had no doubt
Of what Ysengrin was glad about,
So he turned tail and ran flat out.

 Then both Hersent and Ysengrin,
Determined never to give in,
Chased after Renard who stayed ahead,
Despite their speed, so fast he fled
Along a very narrow trail.
1240 Ysengrin could not prevail.

He took a shortcut, but Hersent
Ran on as if she really meant
To catch Renard at any cost,
Knowing that Ysengrin was lost.
She saw the way Renard had taken
And he, looking back, was not mistaken
When he thought her anger was sincere—
To trust her might have cost him dear.
Spurring hard, he kept up his pace
1250   Until he came to Malcrues,* a place
Where he could afford to take a rest.
He disappeared inside, hard-pressed
By his lady, by his erstwhile friend,
Raging, and he did not intend
To greet her with courteous delight.
Reckless in her headlong flight,
She followed Renard when he went inside
Through a corridor that was far from wide.
The castle* was strong and built to last,
1260   And Hersent came plunging in so fast,
Hoping to reach Renard's deep den,*
She got stuck and couldn't back out again.
    And Renard was not inclined to wait.*
He took advantage of her fate,
So that Hersent very nearly died
Between the tunnel and Renard outside,
The tunnel which was much too tight
And Renard shoving her with all his might,
Trying to make his will prevail.
1270   All that stopped him was her tail
That she had drawn so close between
Her legs that nothing could be seen
Of the two apertures underneath.
Renard took the tail between his teeth
And turned it over on her back.
Then all was open to his attack,
And he proceeded to take his pleasure
Joyfully and at his leisure,

Doing whatever he saw fit*
1280   No matter what she might think of it.
Hersent struggled in vain and swore,
"Renard, from now on it is war!"*
And Renard, hearing that, rebounded
So hard that the whole den resounded.
Before he called an end to play
Renard said, in a nasty way,
"My lady Hersent, you thought it best*
Not to put my honor to the test,
And keep hidden what you wanted most
1290   Because, you said, I liked to boast.
And I won't have you made a liar!
To tell the truth is my desire.
What I have done I shall do again,
And say again, seven times or ten!"
Then he proceeded as before
Not stopping to figure up the score.
    And spurring on, last but not least,
Ysengrin gets to the wedding feast,
Close enough to see them celebrate.
1300   Not an instant does he hesitate
But comes out with a mighty yell:
"Renard, I hope you're damned in Hell!
You'll rue the day you did this deed!"
Renard displays no lack of speed,
But says before he takes his leave,
"Lord Ysengrin, it's hard to believe,
When what I did was so well meant,
You'd take it so. Look at Hersent!
I was trying my best to help her out
1310   Of this hole, and all you do is shout
As if your honor were at stake.
Most gracious lord, for God's sweet sake,
Put what I say to any test—
You can see that we both are fully dressed*—
And I swear to you, as I love my life,
I've done nothing improper with your wife.

I'll defend us both from this disgrace—
You need only name the time and place
And I'll state on oath that I haven't lied
1320 So that you and your friends are satisfied."
"On oath! We know how you cheat and lie!
On what kind of oath could we rely?
We'll hear no more idle words and dreams,
Or be victims of your hateful schemes!
And what, indeed, do we have to gain?
In this case the truth is all too plain."
Renard said, "One moment, if you please!
Not everyone, my lord, agrees;
The way you see it is just not right."
1330 "Do you think that I have lost my sight?
That I haven't any eyes in my head?
How on earth could I be misled
About what was happening? Great God above,
When does anyone push and shove,
As I saw you doing to Hersent,
When pulling was really his intent?"
"My lord," said Renard, "one must endeavor
To win, by doing something clever,
What one's strength is not sufficient for.
1340. Madame was stuck in that corridor,
And she is large and rather stout—
How could I hope to pull her out?
She was in the tunnel up to her waist,
But I realized that she was placed
Not far from where it becomes quite wide
A bit further on—that's why I tried
To push her—it was the only way,
Since my leg was injured the other day,
And to pull her was quite beyond my scope.
1350 That is the fact, and I only hope
You won't suppose, as you often do,
That what I say just can't be true. *
And after the lady has been freed,
I don't think that I'll have any need

To defend myself, unless she lies,
Which would come, of course, as a great surprise."
With that Renard set out to reach
His den, having finished his long speech.
Ysengrin is left standing where
1360 He can see Renard regaining his lair,
Renard who has shamed him to his face
And laughed at him in his disgrace.
He did not wait to speak his thought,
But went to help Hersent, still caught—
Her struggles had been to no avail.
Ysengrin grabs her by the tail
And pulls on it with might and main
Until Hersent is in such pain
That Ysengrin in anguish tries
1370 To make the hole a larger size.
He thinks that she is coming unstuck,
And will soon be out, with any luck;
However, when he stands back a bit,
He sees that it's still too tight a fit,
And if his efforts aren't increased,
Hersent will never be released—
He would be sad to lose her so.
Ysengrin, neither lazy nor slow,
Digs and scratches with his claws,
1380 Looking carefully and using his paws
To throw the loosened earth about.
The devil take him or he'll get her out!
When a great amount of dirt was pried
From above, below, and to each side,
He goes to Hersent, tries once more,
She's not stuck as tightly as before.
He pulls her—he doesn't want to fail—
So hard he'd have broken off her tail
If it hadn't been put on to stay.
1390 He feels the tunnel's grip give way
At last, and he's saved Hersent from death,
With just about his final breath. *

Renard and Ysengrin the Wolf

(continued)

Then, as if drunk right out of his mind,*
He kicked her. "Do you think I'm blind,
You vile, stinking, shameless whore—
260   You got what you were asking for!
I saw Renard as he straddled your tail
To cuckold me, and he did not fail!
Now will you say you're innocent?"
Hearing his angry words, Hersent
In her fury nearly lost her head,
But she replied with the truth instead:
"My lord, there's no doubt that I've been shamed,
But I've also been unjustly blamed.
Hear me out and you'll realize
270   That Renard took me by surprise
Against my will. But what's done is done.
It will do no good to anyone
If we just stay here quarreling,
Let's bring our grievance to the king!
That is what Noble's court is for—
Whatever might be cause for war,
Disputes and claims get a hearing there,
And the lion's judgment will be fair.
If we go to him and state our case
280   He will put an end to our disgrace—
You'll meet Renard on the jousting field."*
Ysengrin's anger had to yield

When Hersent explained how she was caught.
"What a fool I was," he said, "to have thought
As I did! But now I've seen the light;
What you advise is surely right.
Renard will pay dearly for his sport
If I can bring him to Noble's court."
   They saw no reason to delay,

290   And stopped for nothing all the way
To King Noble's court where Ysengrin
Was sure of the vengeance he would win
If he could bring his foe to trial:
Renard the Red, despite his guile,
Would find that it was not a joke.
Lord Ysengrin, after all, spoke
Several languages; he presided
As marshal where the king resided.*
Now they had reached the very place

300   Where they hoped the king would hear their case.

At that plenary session* you could find
Creatures of every size and kind*:
Big and little, weak and strong,
And to Noble all of them belong.
There on a rich throne sat the king
With all around him, in a ring,
The mighty lords of his retinue
Each one of whom showed that he knew
The strict decorum that was due
310   A royal court. Then came in view
Lord Ysengrin with his dear Hersent.
They indicated their intent
To address the king and took the floor.
No one would speak a word before
They'd finished. Ysengrin, with a sigh,
Said, "King, your vassals don't comply
With the law. The truth is rarely heard;
None can you trust though he give his word.
According to your royal command,
320   Marriage is sacred in this land;
No one loyal to you would dare
To interfere with a wedded pair.
But Renard doesn't care what you decree:
He has brought to shame my wife and me.
Misfortune follows where he goes.
His deference to you he shows
When he thinks that it is quite all right
To force himself on my wife despite
The fact that he's my relative.*
330   No words of mine could ever give
A true idea of his wickedness.
But I do not speak of my distress,
My lord, to blacken his good name.
Hersent will bear out all I claim."
"Sire, every word my husband said
Is true. Long ago, before I was wed,
Renard already held me dear
And courted me, but I would not hear.

There was no promise and no plea
340   By which he could get me to agree.
Since I've been married to my lord,
I have rejected and ignored
More impertinent attempts to find
Some means to make me change my mind,
And never could he get his way
Until I chased him the other day
Into that hole. I'm big and fat,
So I got stuck, and that was that!
Renard came out of another door
350   And got what he'd been waiting for,
To my dishonor and my shame—
As long as he pleased he played his game.
Lord Ysengrin arrived in time
To witness, in despair, this crime."
Then Ysengrin spoke out again:
"Yes, Sire, that's what was happening when
I caught Sir Renard. What do you say?
Is that how your vassals should obey
The laws you make? When he found Hersent,
360   Was serving justice his intent?
I call the vassals of this land
To witness; my lord king, I demand
That Renard pay for this offense
And also for his insolence
When he paid a visit to my lair,
Pissed on my cubs, pulled out their hair,*
Beat them and let them hear his scorn,
Saying that they were bastards born,
And that I'd be wearing horns for life
370   Because Renard had fucked my wife.
That's what he said, but of course he lied.*
And even after that he's tried
Relentlessly to find some way
To dishonor me. The other day
I was out hunting with Hersent
And that was when, alas, she went

Down the hole that was so tight a fit,
And Renard was making the most of it
When I got there. To my words of blame
380   He said I was wrong: he'd support that claim
On oath; he'd come to any place
I would appoint to state his case.
Now, my lord, it is up to you
To say what compensation's due;
Let it be enough so it would take
A fool to make the same mistake."

Thus Ysengrin for justice pled.
Then King Noble raised his head,
And said, with a little smile, "Before
390   I speak are you sure there's nothing more?"
"No Sire!" he replied. "You cannot doubt
That I grieve to have it talked about,
To the great dishonor of my name."
"Hersent," King Noble said, "you claim
That Renard who's loved you for so long
Has done something you consider wrong,
But I think perhaps you love him too."
"Not I, my lord!" "Then why did you do
Such a foolish thing as to go alone
400   To visit him? That was never known
To be what you'd call a sign of hate!"
"Sire, if you'll let me set you straight,
It was not at all as you suppose.
If the marshal, my dear husband, chose—
Surely you would not doubt his word·—
To speak as you and your lords have heard,
That is because he was in fact
Right there when I was foully attacked."
"Ysengrin was with you?" "Yes, of course!"
410   "You mean that Renard took you by force
With your husband standing there on guard?
By God, believing that comes hard!"
"Sire, if you please," said Ysengrin,
"You are much too eager to begin

Handing down judgments. Wait a while.
If Renard were only here on trial,
Like it or not, what you would hear
Would make the situation clear.
I swear by the loyalty I owe
420   To you, Sire, my argument would show
There's no doubt at all he raped Hersent.
What I said to you before I meant:
I was a witness to the deed—
More proof than that I do not need."
The king always took the greatest care
That his court's proceedings should be fair;
Someone who is of love accused
Should not, for that reason, be abused.
The best of evidence can cheat:
430   Perhaps Renard did not complete
What he began. King Noble thought·
No action really should be brought.
    So when he saw that Ysengrin
Would not give up, being sure he'd win,
He tried to talk him out of it.
"Since it is clear, as you admit,
That Renard pursued Hersent with love,
I would say that he was guilty of
Something less than a mortal sin.
440   Love is the traitor, Ysengrin.
Renard is very brave and clever,
But for all my vassals I endeavor
To be sure that justice will prevail—
The law you appeal to shall not fail."
At Noble's side was a most respected
Camel from Lombardy, selected
By the Pope, who was his friend, to bring,
As legate, tribute sent to the king
From Constantinople. Now, to draw
450   On his understanding of the law,
The king said, "You've been to many places,
Counselor, perhaps you've heard of cases

Involving problems of this kind.
We would be glad, if you don't mind,
To have you, in your wisdom, decide
How justice can best be satisfied."
"*Monsignore,*" he said, "*audite!**
In *Decretalibus, libro tre,*
De concordia officiales
460   *Item matrimoniales*
Quando sunt adulterante
Abscondito or in *flagrante,*
Primo: interrogazione!
If, to the *accusazione*
Responsio does not satisfy,
Ipso facto you reply:
Numquam criminalis sit!
And do unto him as you see fit.
Ergo ego te commendo
470   *Sua fortuna confiscendo*
Let Renard take his *paenitentia*
Mea culpa magna gratia;
Aut, pro bono, lapidation
Aut aflame him to damnation!
Res ipse loquitor,
Rex, what is a ruler for?

Law revilers, *come questo,*
Better to dispatch them *presto.*
By Christ's *corpus,* legislate!
480   Handing judgments wise and straight,
Sia benedicto, monsignore,
By God's Cross, *in tut'onore!*
Never will you be *buon rex*
Unless your *vita* is for *lex*
Like Caesar *sicut sempre* right,
Saying and doing all your might!
Affeczione for your lords!
Or *finito* throne and swords,
Shave off your head and in a cell
490   Monkly pray to serve them well.
Non obstat ruler would you stay,
Justicia is your only way.
Ecco! As you please speak so.
I say no more, no more I know."
    In Noble's court there were two factions,
Opposite in their reactions
To what the Lombard camel said.
Noble the lion raised his head*:
"My wise and valiant lords,* I ask
500   That now you undertake the task
Of giving judgment on this case:
Can love be called a fall from grace
If the lover has not been requited?
If he has, should just one be indicted?"*
When the king had spoken, they all went
Some distance from the royal tent*
To where they could talk in the open air.
A thousand or more assembled there.
Among those least inclined to lag
510   Was my lord Bricemer the mighty stag,
Raging for Ysengrin's sad plight.*
Bruin the bear said he'd delight
In seeing Renard get what he ought.
With them these two allies had brought

Baucent on whose prowess they relied—
Nothing ever made him turn aside.
  Bricemer, leaning against the boar,
When they all asembled, took the floor;
The arguments would now begin. *
520 "Hear me, my good lords! Ysengrin
Has told you how Renard molested
Hersent; as her husband he protested.
He is our cousin and our friend.
But our custom here is to defend
The rights of anyone accused.
Prosecution must be refused
Unless more witnesses can be found
To show there is legitimate ground
For complaint. Without that guarantee,
530 There would be no way for the court to see
On which side innocence belonged,
And someone could be badly wronged.
This I can tell you for a fact:
Ysengrin has never lacked
The power to influence Hersent;
Whatever he asks her, she'll consent.
And she tells a most convincing lie—
On such a witness, who'd rely?"
Bruin spoke up then. "In God's name,
540 My lords, you know I can also claim
The right to give judgment in this case.
To all of you gathered in this place,
I say: the seneschal of our court,
Lord Ysengrin, deserves support.
Were he a traitor or a liar,
A proven criminal, we'd require
More than what his wife could relate
For us to believe his story's straight.
But Ysengrin is so well known
550 That if he brings his wife alone
As witness, we should be content."
"By my faith that's right," said lord Baucent,

"But one thing is not to be denied:
How, on your conscience, do you decide
Which of the two is the better peer?
We all hold friends and kinfolk dear.
If Ysengrin, as you suggest,
Among his neighbors seems the best,
You would certainly find it very hard
560 To get agreement from Renard.
Everyone thinks he alone is shrewd
And valiant also. I conclude
That your argument must be rejected.
All testimony would be respected:
Anyone so inclined could come
And say, 'You owe me a mighty sum'
Attested to only by his wife—
Injustices would then be rife.
That proposal I'll never back.
570 Lord Bruin, you're on the wrong track.
Lord Bricemer, on the other hand—
There's no one wiser in all the land
And none more loyal—just expressed
The point of view that I think best."
"My lords," spoke up Plateaux the deer,
"We have another problem here.
Ysengrin's settlement must include
Full reparation for the food
Renard discovered in his den,*
580 Stole away from him, and then,
When there was nothing left in sight,
Pissed on his children out of spite,
Told them their father's wearing horns
And they are bastards that he scorns;
For this he certainly should be fined.
If Sir Renard isn't so inclined,
And no one can get him to submit,
He'll go on doing just as he sees fit."
Sir Bruin said, "That's true indeed!
590 We are all shamed if we don't heed

73

The fact that Renard could so mistreat
A noble, steal what he had to eat,
And without a scratch get out of there
And wash his hands of the whole affair.
That is what you can call found money!*
Renard couldn't help but think it funny
When his victim appeals and we're so lazy
We do nothing! I think it's crazy
That the king and court just sit there while
600   Renard's behavior is so vile.
But some things slide off and some things stick.
You can't tell a cat whose beard to lick.*
And I'm convinced, with all respect,
That the king won't bother to correct
That scoundrel—we've all seen Noble grin
And add to the wrath of Ysengrin.*
If God would give me the upper hand!
Hear me out, my lords, and you'll understand—
My story won't take long to tell—
610   How Renard made a fool of me as well.

    "That traitor, not many hold him dear,
Discovered one day, while strolling near
A meadow that tall hedges surrounded,
A prosperous village, newly founded.
In a clearing very near the wood,
A certain peasant's dwelling stood,
And he had many a hen and cock
Of which Renard had taken stock.
To this purpose he so set his mind
620   That on more than thirty he had dined.
The peasant and his dogs worked hard
At keeping a watch out for Renard,
And there were traps set everywhere—
No path through the trees without a snare,
Tripwire or noose or woven net—
He used whatever he could get.
This grieved Renard who had no doubt
That if he went in, he might not get out.

And then that devil thought of me,
630   Because I am big and easy to see
While he is very quick and small
So I would be the one who'd fall.
Whether in the woods or in the plain
They were sure to find me without much strain,
And if we travelled as a pair
They would hardly know that he was there;
Straight after me they all would chase,
And he'd be gone without a trace.
He knew that a honeycomb is worth
640   More to me than all else on earth.
And so, in a very friendly way,
This summer, just before Saint John's Day,
'Bruin,' he said, 'wouldn't you be glad
To know where there's honey to be had?'
'Where's that?' 'At Constant de Noen's farm.'
'If I take it, won't I come to harm?'
'Not at all! And I can show you why.'
The wheat crop was already high—
Just the cover we were looking for,
650   And we got in by an open door.
In an orchard with a barn close by,
All day long we had to lie
Without moving, without a sound,
Among the cabbages, close to the ground.*
But then, as soon as the sun had set
And darkness fell, we'd go and get
What we'd come for, break the honeycomb,
Eat what we could and take the rest home.
But that lousy wretch the devil spawned
660   Saw some hens and, impatient, yawned.
He grabbed one. The others clucked in fear.
The peasants couldn't help but hear
And ran, shouting, through the farm.
More than two thousand* heard the alarm
And they all came running toward the yard,
Yelling wild threats against Renard.

When you see forty coming at once,
You are frightened if you're not a dunce!
Galloping with all my might I fled.
670   Renard was already far ahead
On paths and shortcuts he had mapped.
As for me, I was nearly trapped.
   "I caught sight of him at last and cried,
'My lord Renard, tell me why you tried
To run away and leave me behind!'
'Each of us has his way to find,
My dear lord Bruin, let's see some speed!
The old mare trots in time of need.*
If you intend to avoid defeat,
680   Be sure you have sharp spurs on your feet,
Or else a horse that is fit and fleet—
Those peasants would like to salt your meat!
That noise they're making is no joke!
If you feel burdened by your cloak,*
You won't be for long—I foresee no lack
Of helpers to take it off your back.
I'll go ahead—just take a look
At this hen I'm bringing home to cook.

Tell me the sauce that you like best;
690 I'll have it ready as you request!'
With that the traitor dashed away,
Leaving me there to be the prey
Of those whose voices I could hear
Too well, and their dogs were very near.
And then, pell-mell they are on my tail,
Arrows are falling thick as hail,
Peasants are shouting, horns resound
Until their noise seems to shake the ground.
     "Had you been there to hear that sound*
700 And then to see me turn around
And hurl myself against the pack
Of snarling curs and throw them back
Broken and bleeding from my jaws,
Ripped to shreds by my heavy claws,
Then you could say that once at least
You had seen the charge of a mighty beast!
I could have beat them without half-trying,
But with all those barbed arrows flying,
And javelins the peasants cast
710 Falling around me thick and fast,
The most important thing right then
Was to leave the dogs and attack the men,
Rushing at them across the field,
Which they were very quick to yield.
Not one of them was so lion-hearted
But that when I charged him he departed,
Going his way in a frantic run.
But just the same I got hold of one
And hurled him to the ground at my feet.
720 Another, who was in full retreat,
Held a great bludgeon in his fist,
And I couldn't make the first desist
From yelling so that, hearing him shout,
His friend came back to help him out,
And hit me on the top of my head;
Wanting to fight I fell down instead.

I was so weakened by that blow
I had to let my captive go.
I jumped up again; the peasants shouted,
730   And all those dogs that I had routed
Were upon me, tearing at my skin.
The other peasants, hearing the din,
Hasten to increase my woe.
Soon I can feel the stones they throw;
Their arrows and their spears don't help.
Around me the watchdogs bark and yelp—
If one of them comes within my reach
His voice soon rises to a screech;
But I had been too badly hurt
740   And wanted only to desert.
As soon as I was able to pick
A place where the crowd was not too thick,
I started struggling to break through—
It was nearly more than I could do.
But fighting them off, then making a rush,
Up and down hills and through thick brush,
Despite my enemies I could
At last find safety in the wood—
All this because Renard the Red
750   Took a hen between his teeth and fled.
I'm not making a formal complaint.*
I've told this to show Renard's no saint,
Just as we've heard from Ysengrin
And the other day from Tiecelin
Whom he guilefully contrived to pluck.*
Tibert the cat had similar luck
When Renard got him caught in such a snare
That he nearly left his skin right there.
And surely it was a grievous sin
760   To attack the titmouse, his close kin,
Trying to lure her with a kiss—
Judas betrayed God just like this!
Renard's lived in freedom much too long,
And we ourselves do grievous wrong

When a traitor, merciful to none,
Is favored. Justice must be done."
    The bear had spoken for quite a while.
The boar, in his laconic style,*
Answered, "Lord Bruin, this complex matter
770   Won't be resolved by idle chatter.
There is no way to judge the sort
Of complaint that's now before this court
Until the case has been fairly tried.
Who is so clever he'll decide
Which one told the truth and which one lied
When he has only heard one side?
Renard must come and testify,
And then his accusers may reply
And the court will have the final say.
780   Rome wasn't built in a single day.
I am not speaking in defense
Of Renard, but it would make no sense
If attempts to solve this problem led
To fighting among ourselves instead.
That is a crime indeed! This case
Requires that both sides meet face to face
In our presence. We will see our way clear
When we have had a chance to hear
How Renard speaks to Ysengrin's appeal.
790   Until such time as that, I feel
That no decision can be made
As to what compensation must be paid."
    Then said the monkey Cointereau,
"A curse on your head! There's nothing to show*
This is even a criminal affair."
Quick came the answer of the bear:
"Who'd be surprised at your reaction?
You and Renard make just one faction.
It's sure that you know quite a lot
800   About how when he's been on the spot
He's escaped, and he will this time too,
If the judgment's left to him and you."

Cointereau's angry (little he cares
About the growling wrath of bears),
And just to make matters worse replies,
"God save you, master! If you're so wise,
Most humbly I request your grace
To tell me how you'd decide this case."
"By Saint Riche, there's not a single court
810   In the world where they'd allow this sort
Of treachery to go unheeded!
Believe me, our intervention's needed.
Renard is certainly to blame,
Ysengrin has a rightful claim,
And just what are we waiting for?
What does he have to do before
We take action? Don't you all agree
That he's guilty of adultery,
And what's more with one of his close kin!
820   We've heard both Hersent and Ysengrin
Who came here to protest this crime.
And now, without wasting any time,
Renard must be caught. The way to treat
That crook is to bind him hands and feet*
And throw him, just like that, in jail.
Instead of talking, use a flail!
Then take a knife and cut his balls
To be sure no other woman falls
Victim to his wicked lust.
830   Wife or prostitute, it's unjust,
And we must take the greatest care
That next chance he gets he just won't dare.
What becomes of a wedded wife,
Shamed as she's sure to be for life
And grieving because her husband knows?
Certainly Ysengrin's worst foes
Could never think he'd be so unwise,
If he hadn't seen it with his own eyes,
As to speak in public of his shame
840   With Hersent as witness! Support his claim

Or he won't be able to raise his head,
And justice, as I know it, is dead."
The boar said, "This fight leaves none the winner.*
Where is forgiveness for the sinner?
If a nobleman has been accused,
Due compensation won't be refused,
But there must be proof of guilt before
A worthy peace ends a worthy war.
The wolf inspires excessive fright;*
850   Rain falls hard when the winds are light.*
Renard hasn't been convicted yet,
But another chance you may well get.
You've had your say now—who'd deny it?
You'd have done better to keep quiet."

   Lord Bricemer, certainly no fool,
Tried to keep peace, and as a rule
Spoke well of others, unlike the rest.
"My lords," he said, "it would be best
To determine exactly when and where
860   Renard is to come and solemnly swear
To his innocence, as he said he'd do,
And pay what penalty there may be too.
As the monkey stated a while ago,
You can't give judgment unless you know
That the accusation's justified.
Without real proof we can't decide
To fine a man or take his life;
Rather let's try to end the strife.
And we must take the greatest care
870   To be sure the truce is really fair.
One thing especially I'd recommend:
If the king should be away,* let's send
For Frobert La Fontaine's dog Roenel*
To hear the oath—he'll do it well,
And it's our responsibility,
To find someone of perfect probity.
If Roenel could be involved
I think we'd have that problem solved;

If he's willing to accept the task,
880   Everyone will say, 'That's all I ask.' "
Beyond that he didn't have to plead;
The nobles, once and for all, agreed.
    And so the council could adjourn.
With great rejoicing they return
To where King Noble sits in state
With lords assembled, to await
Their decision. As soon as all the rest
Had found their places, Bricemer addressed
The court. He spoke with eloquence,
890   Persuasively, and made good sense,
Being an able rhetorician.
"Lord king," he said, "with your permission,
The council met to find out how,
As the customs of our land allow,
We could find a way to decide this case.
We have an answer, and if Your Grace
Is willing, I've been asked to explain."
The lion's gesture made it plain
That Lord Bricemer should proceed, and so
900   He begins his speech, first bowing low.
    "My lords, hear what I have to say!
If I should make mistakes, I pray
That you'll correct me. Ysengrin
Has a case he is so sure he'll win,
It was clear from his complaint he planned
To get compensation on demand.
But accusations need support,
And he must appear before the court,
Either now or at a time we'll name,
910   With two witnesses to back his claim.
The case must furthermore be tried
Regardless of what was testified
By his wife, right or wrong, for we've observed
That justice will thus be better served.
Bruin and Baucent both tried
To dispute this statement, but on my side

Were many who didn't want it changed.
Now everything has been arranged,
And both parties ought to find it fair.
920 We've decided in what way and where
Renard should swear he's innocent
So that Ysengrin will be content.
All of us were satisfied
To have Roenel the dog preside
On Sunday morning. We'll send word
To Renard that his oath is to be heard
So this argument can be put to rest,
With God's help, in the way we think best."
        Laughing, the lion said to them:
930 "By all the saints of Bethlehem,
If you'd brought a thousand pounds of treasure
You wouldn't have given me such pleasure!
Now I can just keep out of the way
Except for determining the day*
When Renard is to appear and tell
The truth to his good friend Roenel,
Frobert La Fontaine's dog none can pass—
That will be Sunday after Mass.
Renard, of course, will not refuse,
940 But we must be sure he hears the news.
Grinbert the badger will have to go,
On my behalf,* and let him know
That he is to swear a solemn oath
After the recessional. And both
He and Ysengrin must agree
To submit to Roenel's decree."
        From the youngest to those whose hair was white,
They all thought this decision right.
Bricemer and Bruin and Baucent
950 Along with most of the others went
Back to their homes. When the court adjourned,
Grinbert, as he'd been ordered, turned
Toward Maupertuis, Renard's domain.
He found him there and made quite plain

How the noble dukes and counts proposed
That the case should once and for all be closed:
Renard was summoned to appear
To take an oath Roenel would hear;
Renard must clearly understand
960   That he'd have to obey the king's command.
Renard said he asked nothing better;
He'd obey their orders to the letter. *

      Grinbert went straight back to report.
Renard didn't hurry. Once at court
He'd have to watch his step and hide
His thoughts. But he was full of pride,
Not caring how his foes increased,
Nor was he worried in the least
About whether he would lose or win.
970   But his opponent Ysengrin,
Afraid of being disappointed,
Just before the day appointed*
Ran straight to the farmhouse where he saw
Roenel lying on a bed of straw,
Stretching and rolling at his ease,
Close to the hedgerow gate. He flees*
At the sight of Ysengrin, of course,
But there would be a truce in force,
Says Ysengrin in a pleasant way.
980   "Roenel, hear what I have to say!
It's your advice I'm looking for.
Renard and I have been at war
Because he acted to my shame.
I was at court to state my claim,
And Sunday, after Mass, that vile
Traitor is to be on trial,
Unless he finds some way to hide,
And you, Roenel, are to preside.
They tell me the judgment will be fair
990   Because Renard will have to swear
That my family was not abused
And he was wrongfully accused.

The only thing I want to ask
Is that you, as my friend, take on this task*
So what he says must really be true.
It's arranged that what we are to do—
Such was the verdict of the king—
Is find some suitably holy thing
To swear on, but that's beyond my powers."
1000 Roenel replies, "This farm of ours
Is full of relics from the saints
About which there can be no complaints.
There's nothing for you to worry about:
In a ditch near the farm I'll lie stretched out,
And you go back and make it known
That I have choked on a splintered bone,
And that it's certain I am dead.
My tongue will be hanging from my head,
My neck bent back, my teeth exposed.
1010 Near me, the court, as they proposed,
Will assemble for Renard to be tried.
You'll declare that you'll be satisfied
If on my holy tooth he'll swear
To his innocence in this affair.
There'll be no way that I can fail,
If he so much as comes near my tail,
To grab him. Either he takes flight,
Or they'll say, 'That saint can really bite!'
And if he should in fact decline
1020 To venture close enough to the shrine,
He'll find escaping very hard,
For all around him I'll have on guard,
Hidden so they can't be detected,
More than forty of my friends, selected
Because they're experienced and mean.
Renard has skills we have never seen
If the holy relic or the pack
Hasn't strength enough to hold him back.
God save you, do the best you can!"
1030 Ysengrin, having heard this plan,

Wasted no time at all but turned
Toward the forest. He was much concerned
At meeting none of his allies.*
Another worrisome surprise
Was that no message had been sent.
So seeking his friends himself, he went
Deep in the woods and through the plains
Until not a single one remains
Unsummoned. Lord Bricemer, quick to comply,

1040   Arrived at court with his head held high.*
Sir Bruin the bear came running hard,
The boar Baucent and my lord Musard,
The camel,* set out as soon as they heard.

    The lion remembered to send word
To the leopard who lived quite far away,
The panther and tiger don't delay,
Nor does Lord Cointereau disdain
The call, a monkey born in Spain
Who could do magic. Ysengrin

1050   Thought the proceedings could begin
And spoke in a voice that all could hear:
"My lords, you have come from far and near
To attend this trial at my request.
I pray you now to do your best
To be sure the deserving side will win."
Then not only the wolf's close kin*
But the foreigners and each of his friends
Gives his solemn word that he intends
To stay right there at Ysengrin's side

1060   Until he is fully satisfied.
Now that the case has come to court,
They promise him their full support.
All those who owe him fealty
And all his entourage agree.
Thanks to his eloquence he could brag
That many would serve beneath his flag.

    The war banner was carried high
By the skunk whose given name was Spy,*

Tibert the cat, another foe
1070 Of Renard was with him;* but even so
A good many others were allied
With Renard and would support his side.
Sir Grinbert was bound to do his best;
Not only did that great lord detest
Sir Bruin, but as Renard's close kin,
He wanted to help his cousin win.
Rusty the squirrel would also show
His zeal for Renard. He wasn't slow,
And yet his only gait was the trot.
1080 Lady Moire, the woodchuck, would help a lot,
As would Low the mole, and there was Bald,
As the faithful rat was rightly called.
Then came Sir Gallopin the hare,
The dormouse and marten both were there
With the weasel, the hedgehog, and the beaver.
The ferret, who was a true believer,
Made his intentions very clear:
He'd come to fight and he had no fear.
That was a warrior indeed*
1090 To help Renard in his time of need!
 By now there was a mighty throng.
Renard didn't stop to rest as long
As the journey took, and those he led,
Like him, continued straight ahead
To the place appointed for the trial.
Ysengrin had been there a little while.

He and Renard divided their troops
So that in each one there would be three groups.*
Renard on the hillside took his stand;
1100   Ysengrin stayed on the level land,
And, watching the one he longed to attack,
Roenel, with his head bent back,
Lay in the ditch, his tongue extended,
Just in the way he had intended,
Moving neither foot nor head
And looking absolutely dead.
Carefully placed around the edge
Of an orchard whose protecting hedge
Left them completely undetected,
1110   A hundred bitches and dogs selected
For their great prowess and the hate
They felt for Renard were lying in wait.
    Bricemer stepped forward to preside.
No one in all the court denied
That he was entitled to be heard,
For to his wisdom all deferred.
Now, looking out at them all, he stood:
"Renard," he said, "you must make good
The lords' agreement. They deemed it fair
1120   That you should be required to swear
So that Ysengrin is satisfied.
He might, of course, have just relied
On your word without requiring more,
In fact we might almost deplore
His refusal to accept as truth
An oath not taken on the tooth
Of Roenel the Snarling Saint,*
But so you must answer his complaint
That you betrayed him with Hersent.
1130   To prove him wrong, you must consent."
    At that Renard jumps to his feet,
Straightens his clothing so it's neat,*
And gets all ready, nothing loath,
It seemed, to go and swear the oath.

But there was never a stag or deer
With Renard's wits. It was very clear
That he was meant to put his head
In a noose: Roenel was far from dead—
You could see how his whole body shook
1140 With every single breath he took.
What that meant Renard did not inquire;
Bricemer saw him starting to retire.
"Renard," he said, "don't you understand?
You must take the oath with your right hand
On Roenel's tooth, and straightaway."
"My lord, right or wrong, I must obey*
Your commands, and indeed it's my desire
To do whatever you require.
I would not willingly neglect
1150 My duty to you. But with all respect,
You'd find it difficult to believe
The problem that I now perceive—
I wish I could explain, but I'm
More than a little pressed for time."

  Grinbert, Renard's nephew, understood
The trick, and doing what he could,
Spoke to Bricemer in a different way:
"My lord, please hear what I have to say!
My judgment has been often found,
1160 Or at least I hope so, to be sound.
A lord like Renard whose deeds are famed
Should not be made to feel ashamed.

I think it wrong that there's such a crowd
Breathing down his neck—he's much too proud.
These lords will be of more assistance
If they are made to keep their distance.
Clear Renard's way or he'll decline
To swear his oath at the holy shrine."
Bricemer said, "I've been remiss.
1170 You are right; I will attend to this.
Renard should come and go with ease."
He asked the spectators if they would please
Withdraw a little on each side.
For Renard it was easy to decide
What move was right for him to make.
He started out as if to take
The oath in the appointed place,
But then, quickening his pace,
And holding his head up high, instead
1180 That offspring of the devil fled. *
Through an old path hollowed out
Of rock he races; voices shout
And the dogs in ambush start to run.
Now you shall hear me name each one.
    The very first who was all ready
To gallop on with lance held steady*
Was Frobert La Fontaine's dog Roenel;
Robert's Espillar was there as well—
He lived on a rich farm in the region.
1190 After that came the entire legion—
On the heels of those in front they ran—
Harpin and Noisy and Moran,
Hedgehog and with him Peasantbane
And the Snarler, who belonged to Gilaine
(She was Erart the tailor's wife).
The next who raced to join the strife
Were Gorfaut, Breakneck and The Deer,
Follet, Wolfling and Emir.
Macaret Basriver's big hound

1200   Oliver and brave Clermont were found*
        Among the best, and with them, Trumpet,
        Fury, Skeleton and Strumpet.
        The Axe and Pard won't be outdone,
        Nor will Glutton, Brand and The Gelded One;
        Cortin is close behind Rigaut,
        Followed by Lightfoot and Gringaut.
        Lawless, Storm, and Out for Blood,
        Spearbreaker and the one called Stud,
        Tibert de Fresne's best hunting hound—
1210   Over all the field you could hear the sound
        Of his voice, and he'd never lost a race.
        After him took up the chase
        Growler and Pumpkinhead and Dart,
        The Battler, Sheep Herder and Smart,
        And then the heavy-bearded Flail
        And Violet whose voice is frail.
        Then Swallow and Little Cricket came,
        Merlin and the hound called Flame,
        Meadow, Morgan, and with them Whitey,
1220   Right of Way and Beat the Mighty,
        While speeding after them was Ruse,
        Quest and Spur and then Bad News,
        And then Rainbaut the butcher's hound
        Whose teeth are very far from round—
        Should he be fast enough to win,
        There's no way Renard won't lose his skin.
        Then, digging in their spurs, and not
        Far behind are Little Trot,
        Hoptax, Pilgrim, Surprise and Smidge
1230   Coming toward the Audemer Bridge,
        Matching each other stride for stride.
        All these dogs had been long allied
        And formed a single fighting brigade.
        These bitches followed close and bayed
        With enthusiasm, in full cry:
        Crazy Lady and Not Too Shy,

Sibyl and Briar Rose and Crown,
And one who came from out of town.
Behind them galloped Bluette and Fawn,
1240   Chloe, Cleaver, and Cloudy Dawn,
Then came Evil Tongue and Snarl
Who belonged to Robert de la Marle,
Primrose and Spring, last but not least,
The bitch whose master was a priest,
And Lark using all her strength and skill—
She wanted to get there before the kill.
Dodging and twisting, Renard feels
The pack so close upon his heels
He may never make it to his lair—
1250   His life would be forfeit then and there!
And Ysengrin urged on the chase.
If Renard somehow maintained the pace,
It was neither a wonder nor disgrace—
In times of need old mares will race. *
But it didn't do Renard much good:
Just at the edge of a little wood
Four of them caught up with him:
Brumont, Cutting Blade, and Grim. *
Renard inspired them with such hate,
1260   He saw no way to avoid his fate.
He'd always managed to find a way,
Whatever happened, but today
Neither lies nor ruses could prevent
His skin from being badly rent,
And everywhere flew tufts of fur.
So vicious and so fierce they were

That Renard found more than thirteen places
Where their teeth had left deep traces.
But trying to close in for the kill,
1270 They drove and harried him until
With his last strength he shook himself free
At the very door of Maupertuis.

The Trial of Renard

Though his wit and talent did not fail
When Perrot set out to rhyme the tale
Of Renard and Ysengrin, his friend,*
He left out the best part and the end:
The prosecution and defense
As to the guilt or innocence
Of Renard, dragged out, despite his guile,
To Noble's court where he stood trial
For having vilely fornicated
10 With Hersent, as her husband stated.
    The author tells us, in line one,*
That winter had passed, and in the sun
Roses were opening, and bright
Hawthorn flowers, shining white.
The king announced his firm intention,*
Close to the Feast of the Ascension,
That all the animals report
To the palace where he held his court.
Not one would dare let anything
20 Keep him from promptly answering
The lion's urgent proclamation,
Except for Sir Renard, damnation
Take him for a lying thief!
Whom the others said, in their belief,
The king should punish for his pride,
And for the crimes he hoped to hide.
Ysengrin had no objection,
Viewing Renard without affection;
Loudest of all he expressed his ire:
30 "Your majesty, dear gracious Sire,

Grant me justice! Madame Hersent,
Held by Renard with foul intent
In his domain at Maupertuis,
Was forced to commit adultery,*
And he pissed on my poor cubs as well!
That's the latest woe I have to tell.
All of this Renard denied,
And in order that the case be tried
He chose the day when he would swear
40   On holy relics, as is fair.
But somehow he was warned,* and when
We came, retreated to his den.
Why I'm so angry must be clear."
Then said the king, so all could hear:
"Forget about it, Ysengrin—
The only thing that you can win
Is more dishonor to your name.
Counts and kings will play that game,
And nowadays one sees all sorts
50   Of cuckolds, even ruling courts!*
You have little cause, it seems to us,
For making such an awful fuss.
This woe you bring to our attention
Doesn't deserve the slightest mention."
"Most gracious Sire," said Bruin the bear,*
"Is such an answer really fair?
Ysengrin is alive and free,
And if Renard's his enemy,
To seek revenge would not be wrong.
60   You know that Ysengrin is strong;
If Renard lived close to his domain,
And if your sworn peace* did not restrain
All ruled by you from acts of war,
Renard would get what he's asking for!
Of all this kingdom you are lord—
Why don't you put an end to discord,
Put an end to your vassals' fray!
We will hate anyone you say.

Count on us to defend your side!
70   If Ysengrin's dissatisfied
About Renard, let the case be tried;
Let it be judged as you decide.
If one wronged the other, what is due
For that misdeed must be paid to you.*
Send for Renard at Maupertuis;
If you'll entrust that task to me,
And I can find him, there's no doubt
He'll learn what a royal court's about."
As soon as he'd finished, Clamor* roared,
80   "Sir Bruin, a curse on any lord—
Saving your presence—who would say
That the king should let a fine repay
Adultery! Make Renard repent
The shame he inflicted on Hersent!
For other beasts so many times
Have suffered from his filthy crimes,
No one should help him in his need.
Why should Ysengrin have to plead
For justice when Renard attacked
90   His wife so openly the fact
Is known to all? Believe you me,
If he behaved so villainously
And it was my wife he molested,
However strongly she protested,
As far as Maupertuis let him run
But I would make him pay for his fun—
Deep in a muddy ditch he'd groan
Without a sex to call his own!
How could you dream of it, Hersent?*
100   Surely it's something to lament
When Renard who lives without a care
Can boast of mounting you like a mare!"*
The badger* said, "Before it's too late,
Sir Clamor, let us end this debate
Which will otherwise get worse and worse
And beyond our power to reverse.

A malicious tale will soon expand
Until it's entirely out of hand.
And since this case involves no use
110   Of force, no broken door or truce,*
And Renard was prompted by affection,
Why do you make such strong objection?
For a long time he has loved Hersent.
This complaint was never her intent,
And Ysengrin, with little wit,
Is making much too much of it.
Let King Noble and his lords decide
How Ysengrin should be satisfied!
If the baron really has good cause
120   To accuse Renard of breaking laws,*
If he took a walnut not his own,
Then certainly he must atone—
But not until he is here to face
This court for judgment on his case.
However, I think Madame Hersent
Is very far from innocent.
Alas, it does you honor indeed
When your husband has to come and plead
His case where all of us can hear.
130   Truly, if you still hold him dear,
You have already lived too long!
He* fears you not, and you were wrong
To let him* give you a lover's name."
Hersent blushed; she felt such great shame
Her fur stood on end, as with a sigh*
She made the badger this reply:*
"My lord Grinbert, I can bear no more.
All my desire is to end the war
Between my husband and Renard
140   Whose conduct has in no way marred
My honor. Here and now I'd appeal
For the right to prove this by ordeal—
Boiling water, red iron would fail
To burn me—but truth would not prevail.

Alas! I'm doomed to a life of woe.
Why does my lord distrust me so?
I swear by the holy saints above,
And as I hope to deserve God's love,
Renard has had from me no other
150   Kindness than if I'd been his mother.
Don't think I say this to win support
For Sir Renard when he comes to court;
I care for him, and it's simply stated,
Whether he may be loved or hated,
Lose his case or win its dismissal,
As you care for a donkey's thistle.
But jealousy took my husband's wits,
And he thinks the name of cuckold fits!
On Easter day—April first, this year*—
160   As I hold Pinsard, my young son, dear,
For a decade I had lived my life
As Ysengrin's devoted wife.
Everyone came to celebrate
When we were married, a crowd so great,
Such a multitude in den and lair,
That truly you might look everywhere
And not find even so much space
As a goose needs for a nesting place.
Since Ysengrin took me for his own,
170   I have kept my love for him alone—
I'm wronged by this scandalous affair!
So, once again now, I will swear—
And if you don't take me at my word,
At least I will know that you have heard—
By the faith I owe to Saint Marie,
I'm guiltless of debauchery,
And there is nothing I've ever done
That would disgrace a holy nun."
        When they had listened to Hersent
180   Claiming that she was innocent,
Bernard the donkey took the floor.
He believed everything she swore,

Rejoicing to take as proven fact
That Ysengrin's honor was intact.
"Ah me!" he said, "most noble dame,
Would that my spouse were just the same
For loyalty—and everyone,
Dogs, wolves, and women,* under the sun!
For, as I hope God will be kind,
190   Forgive my sins and let me find
Tender thistles where I graze,*
So sure am I that it's not false praise
To say that you would in no measure
Care for Renard or give him pleasure,
Or to his love pay any heed.
But these are wicked times indeed;
The stink of slander fills the air
And people cheerfully will swear
To what was never in their sight,
200   And blame what they should say is right.
Wild Renard, you won't be believed!*
In an evil hour were you conceived
And born. The entire world's persuaded
That you improperly invaded
Madame Hersent. And she'll appeal
For your acquittal by her ordeal.
Say, most noble, gracious king,
Why not put an end to this hateful thing?
On poor Renard bestow your grace!
210   Give me leave to go to his place
And bring him, by safe conduct, back
To answer Ysengrin's attack.
Renard will pay whatever fee
Your court in its wisdom may decree,
And if they find that lack of respect
Caused him to so long neglect
Your summons, for that too he'll pay
Before you let him go away."
"Sire!" the angry lords protest,*
220   "May Saint Giles deny your least request

If you favor Renard to that extent!
Don't have another message sent
To summon him! Let's wait right here
Two more days; if he doesn't appear,
Then have him brought back under guard,
And let his punishment be hard,
Something that he'll remember long."
Noble the king said, "You are wrong
To condemn Renard so out of hand. *

230   I have forces at my command. *
If I am threatened by your pride,
There will be nowhere you can hide!
Renard has a place in my heart still,
Whether you wish him well or ill.
I won't agree to your shameful plan,
If he still wants to be my man.
Ysengrin, as your wife suggested,
Let her innocence be tested,
Or else forget the whole affair."

240   "Don't say that, Sire! It isn't fair! *
What if the red-hot iron is shown
To have burned her fingers to the bone?
Some will learn what they now don't know.
Joy will come to my every foe.
I'll hear their voices loud and clear
Shouting, 'The jealous cuckold's here!'
Let Renard think he's won the game.
I will live with my grief and shame
Until I can do what must be done.

250   But before the harvest has begun
He'll find himself in such a war
No wall or moat or bolted door
Will save him—I will strike him dead!"
"To Hell with that!" King Noble said;
"By Christ's bones, my lord Ysengrin,
Is that a war you think you'll win?
Can you really do as you have claimed?
Will Renard be either dead or maimed?

By the faith I owe to Saint Lenard,
260   With all the tricks known to Renard,
It's much more likely he won't fail
To do you in than you prevail.
Anyway, what can be the use
Of discussing it? We've sworn a truce,
And all the land has been brought to peace.
Woe to the guilty if that should cease!"
    Ysengrin, when the king had spoken
Of his concern lest the truce be broken,
Was so upset and in such dismay
270   He didn't know to what saint to pray.
He sat near the benches on the ground;
Between his legs his tail was wound.*
Renard would have much to celebrate
If God had meant him for that fate:
With the king determined to achieve
The peace whoever that might grieve,
Renard and Ysengrin could no more
Incite each other to make war.
But Chanteclere and Pinte his hen
280   Were arriving at the court just then
With three others all of whom
Want justice for their sister's doom.
Now the fat is in the fire,*
For Chanteclere, that noble sire,
And Pinte, whose eggs have such a span,
And Blacky, Whitey, and Roseanne,*
Had brought with them a little cart
With curtains that they drew apart.
The others saw, as they came near,
290   A litter on which, as on a bier,
A hen was lying. She'd been caught
By Renard whose cruel teeth had wrought
Such harm her leg was a splintered shred,
And one of her wings hung by a thread.
    King Noble felt that he had earned*
A rest, and court should be adjourned;

But all at once the hens appear,
Wringing their hands,* and Chanteclere.
First of all Pinte begins to plead,
And the others loudly take her lead:
"Most gracious beasts, for God's sweet sake,*
You dogs and wolves,* do not forsake
A poor creature so forlorn!
I curse the day that I was born!
Oh come, make haste and take me, Death,
Since Renard won't let me draw a breath
In peace. I had, on my father's side,
Five brothers—every one supplied
A dinner for Renard, the thief
Who has brought me to such bitter grief.
Not counting me, my mother gave birth
To five young virgin hens whose worth
For Gonbert del Frenne* would well repay
His fattening them to make them lay.*
Oh! How I wish he'd kept his grain!
He fed them well, and yet the gain
Went to Renard, for all but one
Had passed through his throat when he was done.
And you who are lying in the bier,
My sister sweet, my friend so dear,
So tender and so plump, alas!
How wearily the days will pass
Without you—in sorrow I must dwell.
Renard, I hope you burn in Hell!
Not a moment can we turn our backs
Without the fear of your attacks—
Chased and mauled, your victim's pressed
Against the wall as you rip her vest!*
I came out yesterday and found
My poor dead sister hurled to the ground,
And Renard so far away from the place
That Gonbert could not have given chase
On foot, and he has no swift horse.
That's why I've come here. But no force

300

310

320

330

Can bring to justice one who grins
At threats, and doesn't care two pins
For anyone's wrath." She said no more,
Poor Pinte, but fell straight down on the floor.
They saw she had fainted dead away,*
340 And next to her the other three lay.
To get the ladies up on their feet,
Each dog and wolf rises from his seat,
And helped by the other beasts, they pour
Buckets of water on all four.

    Just as soon as they'd recovered,
As in my source book I discovered,*
They went where King Noble had his seat
And fell on their faces at his feet.
Meanwhile the kneeling Chanteclere
350 Wet the king's feet with many a tear.
When Noble saw Chanteclere, in truth
He felt such pity for the youth,*
That nothing on earth could make him hide
His feelings; from his depths he sighed,
Then raging, lifted up his head.
The bravest beast could not have said—
Not even the mighty bear or boar—
He felt no fear at the lion's roar.
Coward the hare heard it and quivered,
360 Two whole days in a fever shivered.*

All the courtiers shook as one.
By their terror they were quite undone.
King Noble, lifting his tail up high,
In rage and anguish gave a cry
So loud that the house walls nearly broke,
And when the echoes died he spoke:
"My lady Pinte," the emperor said,
"I swear on my dead father's head—
His daily alms from me are still due—
370   I feel great sympathy for you,
And wish somehow to relieve your woe.*
Renard shall come if he will or no!
By what you shall see with your own eyes,
Hear with your ears, you'll realize
How truly justice has been done.
Vengeance I'll have on anyone
For breaking the peace and murdering!"
    Ysengrin, when he heard the king,
Leaped to his feet exclaiming, "Sire!
380   Actions of valor must inspire
Great praise. It will be a noble deed
If you can help poor Pinte in her need,
And get revenge for Madame Copee,
Mangled and butchered as we see.
I do not say it because I hate
Renard, but in sorrow for her fate;
Not out of hatred, but I resent
The slaughter of the innocent."
The emperor replied, "My friend,
390   My heart is heavy. Times without end
Renard's misdeeds have cost us dear.
To you and to the strangers* here
I say the adulterer can't hide*
From the consequences of his pride;
He broke the peace that I proclaimed,
And by his actions I am shamed.
But now there is another affair
We must attend to. Bruin the bear,

I ask you to put on your stole,*
400   Commend to God the poor hen's soul!
And you, Lord Clamor, by my command,
Shall dig a grave in that ploughed land."*
"As you will, Sire," replied the bear,
And he went quickly to prepare
The several things that he would need.
Meanwhile, their ruler in the lead,
The other council members started
The vigil for the dear departed.
They heard Lord Slow the snail intone
410   Three whole lessons all on his own,
Bricemer the stag and the dog Roenel
Sang verse and responses very well.

    The service lasted through the night,
But when the sun gave its first light,
The burial could not be delayed.
First, in a casket that was made
Fit for a king, and all of lead,
They reverently placed the dead.
They buried her beneath a tree
420   With a marble stone in memory
Of Madame Copee and to extol
Her deeds and to God commend her soul.
Carved with a chisel or else a knife,
This epitaph summed up her life:
"Here on this plain, beneath this tree,
Lies Pinte's sister, Madame Copee.
Renard, who pursues his evil ways,
With cruel teeth cut short her days."
Whoever witnessed poor Pinte's crying,*
430   Cursing Renard for her sister's dying,
And Chanteclere with his feet stretched out,*
Would pity them, I have no doubt.

    When grief had lost its violence
And mourning was not quite so intense,
The lords cried, "Emperor, it's time
That you made that thief pay for his crime!

We're tired of his tricks, and it's no use
Hoping that he'll respect a truce."
"Yes," says the king, "that's all too true.
440   Brother Bruin, here's a task for you—
There's nothing at all for you to fear*—
Tell Renard that I have been here
Waiting for him three whole days."
"Gladly," says Bruin. He delays
Not for a moment but mounts and rides*
Toward the forest where Renard resides,
And, never stopping, on he went.
Meanwhile there was a great event,
As through the valley Bruin rode,
450   Back at the court, and it would bode
Ill for Renard. Sir Coward the hare,
Who'd caught such a fever from his scare
(Two days he was in a shivering fit),
Had now, thank God, been cured of it.
Here's how he found the remedy:
Not wanting to leave Madame Copee,
Above the martyr's grave he lay,
Fell fast asleep, and was cured that way.
Ysengrin, when he heard the story
460   Of the new martyr's proven glory,
Said that he had an awful earache,
And then, deciding he would take
Roenel's advice,* he put his head
Upon the grave and was cured, he said.
Were it not good doctrine that about
A miracle one can have no doubt—
And there was Roenel to provide
A witness—they would have thought he lied.
    When they listened to this new report,
470   Some were happy at the court,
But Grinbert thought it bad indeed.
He and Tibert the cat,* who plead
On Renard's behalf, fear that the news
Means that without a mighty ruse

Renard's in a bad way if he's caught.
And a shortcut had already brought
Lord Bruin through the depths of the wood
To where Renard's great fortress stood.
Bruin would have to shrink before
480   He found a way inside the door*—
At the barbican he has to stay.
Renard, who takes the world for his prey,
Had his inner lair dug very deep,
And just then he was fast asleep.
He had provisions in his den:
There was a beautiful plump hen;
And two chicken legs down to the feet
That morning had left him quite replete.
Now, as if he meant to ruin
490   Renard's sweet slumber, here comes Bruin!
"Renard," he says, "it's Bruin the bear,
Sent by the king. Come out of there!
Come out and talk to me where I stand,
And I will tell you the king's command."
Renard saw enough to recognize
Bruin the bear by his great size,
And, in an instant, he had planned
A way to get the upper hand.
"Good Bruin, as I hold you dear,
500   I'm sorry they sent you way down here

107

On a useless errand—it's a shame.
I would have left before you came
Except that I was disinclined
To leave a good French meal behind.
You know how a wealthy man is treated:
'Sir, will you wash?' is the way he's greeted
When he comes to court; everyone believes
It's an honor just to hold his sleeves.
They serve him beef cooked with vinegar,
510   Then ask him which he would prefer
Among the many other dishes.
Who listens to a poor man's wishes?
They think he's made of a devil's shit.
Not by the fireside does he sit;
For a table he must use his lap
As the housedogs crowd around and snap,
Snatching the bread out of his fingers.
Over a single drink he lingers,
Knowing they won't refill his glass,
520   And once will the serving platter pass.
Boys will shower him with bones
Drier than red-hot burning stones. *
Each holds his bread clutched in his hand. *
The tables of the lords of the land
Miss what seneschals and cooks withhold,
All of them cut from the self-same mold. *
Would they were burned and their ashes blown!
Whatever they want they take for their own;
Meat and bread from the master's stores
530   Go to make dinner for their whores.
All this is why I wouldn't have cared,
Good my lord, to travel unprepared,
And this noon I have not only dined
On good peas and bacon well combined,
But ate every bit I had at home
Of fresh new honey in the comb."
"*Nomini Dame, file Christom!*" *
The bear said, "Honeycomb! Where's it from?

By the bones of Giles the blessed saint,
540   My belly so craves it I feel faint!
God's heart! Dear gracious lord, please say,
Mea culpa! that you'll show the way!"
Renard sticks his tongue out with a look
That says the bear is on the hook,
And, all unknown to the poor Bruin,
Prepares to bring his victim in,
Carefully coiling his long line:
"Bruin, if you were a friend of mine,"
Renard said, "if I only knew
550   That I really could depend on you,
Then, by my son Rovel, I swear
This very day I'd take you there.
You'd be standing at the honeyed site,
Filling your belly with delight.
In Lanfroi the forester's domain,
Not far from here, rich combs remain.
But near or far, what does it matter?
All this is only idle chatter.
You, if I served you as a guide,
560   Would take it out of my poor hide."
"Renard, how can you distrust me so!"
"I do." "But why?" "What I know I know.
There's an evil purpose in your heart."
"Renard, it must be the devil's art
That makes you think I could be so vile."
"All right. I'll give your good faith a trial. *
I would not wrong you, nor you me."
"That's the truth! For by the fealty
I swore to Noble, our gracious king,
570   Never would I do anything
To harm you; never do I intend
To treat you other than as my friend."
"Those are the words I wanted to hear,
Bruin, and now I have no fear."
When they had come to this agreement,
Happy for both, away they went

On their good chargers, the two abreast,
And galloped, never taking a rest,
So urgently did they wish to gain
580   Lanfroi's forest, where they drew rein.
There an enormous oak tree stood.
Lanfroi, who wanted to sell the wood,
Had driven in two mighty wedges,
Making a slit between their edges.
Renard said, "Bruin, my dear friend,
We have come to our journey's end.
The honey's inside there. Eat it first,
Then we will go and quench our thirst;
You shall have what you've always loved."
590   Standing on his hind legs, Bruin shoved
His muzzle and his two front paws
Into the hole. To help his cause,
Renard keeps pushing him from below,
Shouting he hasn't far to go:
"Open your mouth, you son of a whore!
You're almost there! Just a little more!
Only unlock your teeth, you scum!"
Now Renard's great moment has come;
For Bruin, though, it's not so funny—*
600   He didn't find a drop of honey
However hard and long he tried,
And, while his mouth was opened wide,
Renard, damn his soul! with a mighty clout,
Suddenly knocked both wedges out!
In the space where the oak tree had been split,
A third of Bruin was tightly fit—

Not a good way to take a rest!
The poor bear really is hard-pressed,
Held a captive by the tree,
610   While Renard (not known for charity,
And let his confession not be made)*
Shouts that it's he who's been betrayed:
"Bruin, I always did believe
That you had something up your sleeve!
You're at the honey and won't stop
Until you've left me not a drop!
Next time I'll beat you at your game!
But don't you feel the slightest shame
At eating all that lovely honey?
620   And then, I suppose, I'll get no money!
I can imagine the kind of trick
You'd have played on me had I fallen sick—
You'd have brought rotten pears* for a treat!"
But Renard knew he had better retreat
When he looked up just in time to see
That Lanfroi was coming toward the tree.
The peasant* could not believe his luck—
There was Bruin so tightly stuck!
Off to the village Lanfroi sped,
630   Shouting, "Come help and the bear is dead!

D ont on peult faur une bourfe
et unfi fen ua li filz alourfe

We've got him now but hurry! hurry!"
You should have seen the peasants scurry,
Swarm through the trees with bloodthirsty looks!
Some carry clubs, some pruning hooks,
Flails and axes raised to attack!
Bruin shivers, fears for his back.

    Hearing the mob's ferocious voice,
He knows in his heart he has no choice—
Better, no doubt, to sacrifice
640   His muzzle, held as in a vise,
Than to wait there for Lanfroi to seize.
So Bruin starts to push and squeeze
And pull, no matter how it hurts,
Stretching his skin while blood spurts
In bright streams from his broken veins.
His skin gives way—not enough remains
On his mangled head to make a purse—
Never did any beast look worse!
From all his dreadful wounds the blood
650   Comes pouring in a crimson flood;
There's no skin at all on his front feet.
Much has he suffered to retreat!
But now at last poor Bruin could
Run away through the depths of the wood.
And the shouting peasants are not slow:
The son of Lord Billin, called Bertot,
And with him Hardoin Hit and Run,
Gonbert and with him Gallon's son
(Falcon's nephew) and Count Ortrands
660   Who strangled his wife with his own hands;
Tygers, who baked the village's bread—
(Black Cornelia he took to bed).
And Aymery the Sickle Breaker,
And Rocelin the son of Shaker.
Ogier's son, not there to relax,
Held in his hand a battle-axe;
And there was my lord Hubert Grosset
And the son of Faucher Galopet.

The war party was increased
670   By the presence of the parish priest,
Father of Martin de la Tour.
He had just finished spreading manure
And took up the pitchfork he had plied
To plant it deep in Bruin's side
As the bear in pain and anguish fled—
A little deeper and he was dead.
Catching Bruin against an oak,
Another of those peasant folk,
A comb and lantern maker by trade,
680   Struck at him, not with a blade,
But with a steer's horn, wrenching his back.
Besides all these, there is no lack
Of peasants beating him with flails—
The wonder is that he prevails.
Renard, who knows his prospects are grim
If Bruin gets a chance at him,
Hears the bear at a distance, free,
And takes a shortcut to Maupertuis,
That mighty fortress where he knows
690   He'll be safe from his strongest foes.
Seeing Bruin close to his door,
Renard gibes at him once more:
"Bruin, I hope you're satisfied!
I know you never meant to divide
Lanfroi's honey. Those who pretend
Good faith will come to a bitter end,
And don't think a priest will see you through!
But tell me, are you aspiring to
A monastic order? What's this red
700   Hood-like thing that's on your head?"
But Bruin, too far gone for banter,
Left at an energetic canter,
Still in terror at the thought
Of what would happen if he were caught.
    So he spurred on, so fast that soon,
Just as the bells were rung at noon,

The bear was riding through the gate
To where the lion sat in state.
Bruin fell fainting on the floor,
710   His face entirely covered with gore.
As his friends come running, it appears
The bear has arrived without his ears.
The king said, "Bruin, who did that?
Who so foully ripped off your hat
And left your legs in such a state?"
His loss of blood had been so great
That Bruin's voice was very weak:
"King," he said, "I went out to seek
Renard, and found him, as you can tell."
720   Then at King Noble's feet he fell.

    You should have heard the lion roar,
Tearing his mane out as he swore
On Christ's pure heart what he would do!
"Bruin," he says, "I think you're through. *
You've been murdered, but it won't be long,
By the death of Christ, before this wrong
Is avenged. Renard will pay so dear
No one in France will fail to hear!
Where are you, Tibert? Be on your way
730   To Maupertuis, and with no delay!
Tell that red-haired bastard I command
That before the nobles of this land
He make the reparation due.
And that won't be accomplished through
Gold and silver, nor is there hope
That words will cut down the gallows rope
Waiting for the killer we accuse!"
Tibert, could he have dared refuse,
Would still not have come to Maupertuis,
740   But there's no way out; he must agree
With what the king and council decide.
So the cat, who doesn't ride astride,
Gallops along the valley floor,
Spurring his mule—and there's the door

Behind which he will find Renard.
He prays to God and to Saint Lenard,
Who oftentimes has captives freed,
That he, by his prayers, would intercede
And keep Tibert safe from his old friend,
750 For he is sure Renard would contend
With the devil to do an evil deed,
So dear to him is the holy creed!
Something increased his consternation
Just as he reached his destination:
Between an ash tree and a pine
He saw a buzzard.* He made a sign,
And said to it, "Go right! Go right!"
But the bird kept on its left-hand flight.
For quite some moments Tibert paused.
760 It was most of all the bird that caused
The cat to think he'd be defeated,
Shamed and very badly treated.
Tibert, by gloomy thoughts inspired,
Felt that he was not required
To ask if he could go inside.
He went just up to the door and tried
To do his errand tactfully;
No good came of it, as you shall see.
"Renard," he said, "as I hold you dear,
770 Tell me, at least, if you are here."
Renard seemed not to reply at first;
Out of sight, between his teeth, he cursed:

a riens q plus le deconforte

"Tibert, my friend, you'll rue the day
You ever put yourself in my way!
I'll have your hide right down to the bone!"
Then he said, in a normal tone:
"*Welcomme,** good Tibert, to my home!
If you were on your way from Rome
Or from Compostela,* I'd hold you dear
780   And be as glad to see you here
As to welcome the Pentecostal feast!"
It doesn't hurt Renard in the least
To offer greetings of that sort.
Tibert's reply is rather short:
"Renard, please understand one thing:
I'm only here to speak for the king—
It's certainly not the way I feel—
And he condemns you without appeal.
Grinbert, your cousin, takes your side,
790   But with no one else are you allied—
What the others feel for you is hate."
Renard is not inclined to debate:
"How I deal with threats you shall see,
And those who'd sharpen their teeth on me.
While I can I will live my life!
I'll go to court and settle this strife,
If they dare accuse me to my face."
"That will be very wise, your Grace;
For this, as always, you have my praise.
800   But I've had nothing to eat for days—
My spine is bent just like a bow.
Haven't you something down below,
A hen or a rooster I could taste?"
Renard said, "That would be a waste.*
Everyone knows the way you steal
Plump mice and rats to make a meal—
Poultry is not the thing for you!"
"Oh yes it is!" "That can't be true."
"I'll eat until the last hen's gone."
810   "All right. Tomorrow, before the dawn,

You'll be full where you now are hollow.
I'll go first, and you just follow."
   With that Renard came out of his lair.
Tibert followed him, unaware
That he was already caught by guile.
They saw a village after a while
Where for sure you'd be hard-put to find
A coop where Renard had never dined.
"Tibert," he says, "you're in for a treat.
820   In one of the houses on that street,
Lucky for us, there lives a priest—
I know him well, to say the least.
His oats and barley would well suffice
Except that he is plagued by mice
Who take such pleasure in that fare
It was nearly gone when I was there.
I set out to capture a hen—
Before I knew it, I'd taken ten!

C-fu cummamaurws nor
aucli temps eft fens Hc
f1 coin eftoit la centfion
auc renait ten en fame

Five of them I ate today;
830   The others I put safely away.
Just inside is the hiding-place,
So go right in and stuff your face!"
That treacherous master of deceit
Was lying. Neither oats nor wheat
Were kept in the place where Tibert went,
A fact the priest did much lament.
The whole village used to deplore
The way the priest's light-fingered whore,
The mother of Martin de la Tour,
840   Took all he owned. I am quite sure
He had no oxen, not a cow—
His barnyard was reduced by now
To just two chickens and a cock.
Young Martin, who later wore the frock,
And then would choose monkish robes to wear,
Had closed the entrance with a snare,
Hoping to catch the foxy beast.
God had most greatly blessed the priest
With a son to think of tricks like that,
850   And so outwit a fox or cat!
Renard says, "Tibert, my dear fellow,
Go help yourself, unless you're yellow!
I'll be waiting for you right outside."
Tibert sets forth in a running stride
And then his neck is in the noose—
There seems no way to get it loose!
He knows he's done a stupid thing—
The more he pulls, the tighter the string.
He struggles—surely something can be done!
860   But here comes Martin on the run
Yelling, "Father! Oh, make haste!
Help me, Mother! There's no time to waste!
Come to the hole and bring a light—
We'll have some sport with the fox tonight!"*
    At this young Martin's mother awakes,
Jumps up, lights a candle, and she takes

Her spindle with her. At Martin's calls
The priest, holding on to his balls,
Leaps out of bed, and runs still faster.
870 For Tibert it's a real disaster:
He carries more than a hundred blows
Away with him when at last he goes.
The priest strikes, and his concubine,
And both of them are doing fine
When Tibert, in his struggle, spies
What's dangling between the priest's thin thighs,
And grabs—this is told in all the books—
With teeth and claws like grappling hooks,*
And hangs on until it is off for good.
880 As soon as the woman understood
The full extent of the tragedy,
Three times she cried, "Alas for me!"
And when she would have made it four,
She swooned and fell down upon the floor.
This gave young Martin such a scare
That the cat, who'd bitten through the snare,
Could take advantage of the uproar
And run until he was safe once more.
Tibert has had some satisfaction—
890 Ah! could he now go into action
Against the cause of his rage and pain!
But Renard hadn't chosen to remain.

When he saw Tibert in the snare,
He was on his way right out of there,
Having no desire to come to harm;
He heard young Martin sound the alarm
And went home—he didn't even wait
To see what would be poor Tibert's fate.
"Ah! Renard, Renard," Tibert said,
900   "May God not take you when you're dead!
But I deserve to be badly treated,
Having so often been defeated
By that lying cheat, Renard the Red!
May the cuckold priest have little bread
And a wretched place to lay his head,
He and the whore he takes to bed,
For what they've done to me today!
But at least he won't be able to play
The parish music very well
910   Since he's been left with just one bell.
And as for Martin de la Tour,
I hope he'll be forever poor
And that, for giving me such blows,
His lifetime will not come to a close
Before he's a monk with no relief
Until he's hanged for a proven thief!"
    So in a rage at his disgrace,
He came through the valley to the place
Where the king sat in his judgment seat.
920   Tibert saw him, fell at his feet,
And told him his fantastic tale.
"God!" said the king, "My powers fail.
My lords, I am extremely shocked
To find my dignity so mocked.
And where's the champion I need
To take revenge for Renard's foul deed?
My lord Grinbert, I'm half-inclined
To see your influence behind
The way Renard despises me."
930   "I swear, Sire, that could never be!"

"Then go and bring Renard to court.
If you fail, don't bother to report."
"Sire," said Grinbert, "it can't be done.
That bastard would just think it fun—
He'd never yield to my desire,
Unless I had a letter, Sire.
By Saint Israel, no appeal
Would move him, but if he saw your seal,
He'd know, whatever pretext he used,
940   There's no way for him to be excused."
"My dear Sir, that makes very good sense."
Noble then dictated the contents
While Baucent wrote down everything;
He sealed the letter for the king.

    Then Grinbert, with the king's permission,
Started out to perform his mission.
Through meadow and wood he went; no lack
Of sweat was pouring off his back,
And still he had far to go before
950   He would be close to Renard's front door.
At vespers he came upon a lane,
And at nightfall found Renard's domain.
The walls rose high above his head;
There were narrow passageways that led
To where he found a low-vaulted door
Into a courtyard. Then, still more*
Afraid of what Renard would do
If he should hear him coming through,
He hugged the walls and waited to see—
960   That was Grinbert at Maupertuis.
As soon as his visitor had stepped
Onto the turning bridge* and crept
Along the passageways—even then,
Before Grinbert came into his den,
Hindquarters first and head to the rear,
Renard knew who was coming near.
He welcomed Grinbert with warm delight,
Wrapped both arms around him tight,

And two soft pillows behind him pressed,*
970   Because his cousin was his guest.
I think Grinbert was very wise
To keep his message for a surprise
Until he'd had enough to eat,
But after dinner, feeling replete,
"My lord," he said, "everyone knows
The way you lie and cheat—it shows.
I'm here to tell you the king demands,
No, not demands—the king commands
That at his palace you submit
980   To whatever sentence he deems fit.
Why wage a war you cannot win?*
What did you want of Ysengrin?
Why harm Tibert? Why hurt Bruin?
You have betrayed them to your ruin.
I'd like to offer you some cheer,
But I think your time to die is near,
And all your children will share your fate.
Break this seal and you'll get it straight.
Just read the words that are written here."
990   Renard listens, and shakes with fear.
He trembles, as he breaks the seal,
For what that gesture may reveal.
He reads the first few words and sighs,
Well understanding what meets his eyes.
    "Noble the lion, whose majesty
Prevails throughout these lands where he
Over all the beasts is king and lord,
Promises Renard he cannot afford
To ignore this summons: he'll pay dear
1000   If tomorrow he does not appear
To make amends for his misdeeds.
Not silver and not gold he needs,
And let no champion give him hope;
He'll pay his debt with a hangman's rope."
    A terrible message for Renard!
Inside his chest his heart beat hard,

His face took on a somber hue.
"For God's sake, Grinbert, what shall I do?
Pity a poor defenseless captive!
1010 Alas that I have this hour to live,
If I must hang until I'm dead
Tomorrow. I wish I'd been instead
A monk at Cluny or Citeaux!
But many of them are false, and so
I'd soon have wanted to depart;
In that case better not to start."
"You've other things to worry about!"
Said Grinbert. "And while you're here without
People around you, I suggest
1020 That it would be well if you confessed.
Confess your sins to me at least—
Since I don't see any closer priest."
"My lord Grinbert," Renard replies,
I think your counsel very wise;
I'm close to death for my transgression,
And if you hear my true confession
I've nothing at all to lose thereby,
And I am saved if I have to die.
    Listen! I heartily repent
1030 For what I did with Dame Hersent
Who is the wife of Ysengrin.
She tried to cover up that sin
But no one believed her—that was shrewd
For she was well and truly screwed.
May God preserve my soul from Hell,
So many time I rang her bell—
Mea culpa!—if I have to face
Ysengrin, I'll lose the case.
How to deny that he's been cheated,
1040 Three times imprisoned and defeated!
Now I will tell you all about it.
I made him fall into the pit
Just as he carried off a sheep.
Lucky for him he got to keep

Any skin at all, for it was shed
In a hundred blows before he fled.
When I had trapped him as I planned,
There were three shepherds close at hand
Who beat him like a balky ass. *

1050   Another time I helped him pass
Through an entrance to a rich man's larder,
But getting out was a great deal harder,
For his belly swelled still more with each
Of three hams he found within his reach.
I set him to fishing through the ice;
His tail was caught as in a vise.
I made him fish in a pool one night
When the full moon was very bright,
And its reflection, white and round, *

1060   Looked like a lovely cheese he'd found.
So once again I had my wish—
He ended up on a load of fish.
A hundred times I took him in
With the guileful schemes my wits can spin.
Thanks to me he had a tonsured head. *
Then he saw how well the canons fed
And thought their life wouldn't be so hard;
Those fools gave him their sheep to guard!
I could talk all day and not be done

1070   Telling you how I had my fun.
There's not one beast in Noble's court
Who wouldn't give me a bad report.
When I led Tibert into the net
He thought that it was rats he'd get. *
In all Pinte's family there lives
One aunt; her other relatives,
Cocks and hens alike, were able
To fill a place at my dinner table.
When a cow and ox and the mighty boar

1080   With other beasts stood at my door
Well armed, Ysengrin, in the lead,
Was sure that he had all he'd need

To win. There were on his side as well,
With the watchdog, Loudmouth Roenel,
Seven times twenty dogs and bitches
All of whom soon needed stitches,
Having most foully been betrayed—
I'd gotten to everyone they paid.*
I certainly have no cause to boast
1090 Of how I routed that great host—
Only by guile were they defeated.*
I watched as long as they retreated
And in salute stuck out my tongue.
God! What I did when I was young!
But now, *mea culpa!* true remorse
Turns my life from its sinful course."
"Renard, Renard," Grinbert begins,
"I've heard the confession of your sins
And all the evil you have done.
1100 Your trial, by God's will, may yet be won.
Take care from now on to do no wrong."
"May God not let me live so long,"

Renard replied, "that all my ways
Are not deserving of His praise."
He shows a pious resolution,
Kneels, and Grinbert gives absolution
In French* and in the tongue of Rome.
Next morning, before Renard left home,
He kissed his children and his wife,
1110   All of them fearing for his life.
When the time of separation came,
"My sons," he said, "defend our name!
However this misadventure goes,
Protect my castles against our foes.
Against a count, against a king,
For months you won't need to fear a thing—
No count or baron, no lord* would dare
Rob your head of a single hair.
You'll never be so much as grazed,
1120   If you keep every drawbridge raised
And are well provisioned—for seven years*
You'll stand them off and have no fears.
What more is there for me to say?
I commend you now to God, and pray
That He will bring me back once more."
With that he knelt down on the floor;
Because he would have to leave his lair,
Renard began to say a prayer.
    "God, King, in your omnipotence,
1130   Let my craft and my common sense
Not be lost to me out of fear
When before the king I must appear
To answer Ysengrin in court.
Whatever he chooses to report
Let me make it harmless to admit,
Or find some way of denying it;
And let me come back to Maupertuis
Alive and well, so that I may be
Avenged on those who seek my disgrace."
1140   Renard fell down upon his face,

Then, beating his breast for what he'd done,
Made the sign against the evil one.
    And now the noble lords will go
To court; on their way swift rivers flow;
There are narrow trails to follow past
High mountain ridges until at last
They ride across a level plain.
Renard is really feeling the strain;
That's why, in the woods, they go astray
1150   And find no footpath, road or way
Until, where farmland had been cleared,*
A barn that belonged to nuns appeared.
Surely one would find inside
The best of what the world can provide:
Cheese and milk and lambs they keep,
Geese and oxen, cows and sheep,
And young ones they fatten up to eat.
"Come on!" said Renard. "Don't drag your feet!
Now I can see where we went wrong.
1160   There's underbrush to follow along
To the henyard, then it's straight ahead."
"Renard, Renard," the badger said,
"Does God not know what you say that for?
Foul unbelieving son of a whore,
Stinking glutton—I thought you craved,
Pleading for mercy, to be saved!

127

I heard your confession, did I not?"
Replied Renard, "I quite forgot.
I'm ready now. Let's go on like friends."
1170   "Renard, Renard, it never ends!
God himself you will try to trick!
On you repentance can never stick.
How you came to be so mad, God knows!
Your life may be coming to a close,
And scarcely have you confessed before
You turn around and sin once more.
Evil has marked you out as prey.*
Let's go now. A curse upon the day
When you were severed from your mother!"
1180   "You do very well to say so, brother!
But now let's go our way in peace."
To make his cousin's scolding cease
Renard was keeping very quiet
As to the farm—he dared not try it,
But he craned his neck a little when
He caught a sight of a lovely hen,
Sadly thinking he'd rather have fed
And paid the price, though it were his head!
    As the two lords proceed with their ride,
1190   Grinbert's mule* has a mighty stride,
But fear of his master's wrath* so grips
Renard's horse that he constantly trips;
Beneath his skin the blood pounds hard,
So greatly does he fear Renard.
They run through fields, through woods they scramble,
Galloping or at an amble,
Over the mountain pass they ride
To the valley on the other side
Where those accused are called to account;
1200   In front of the great hall they dismount.
    As soon as it's known Renard is there
Everyone hastens to prepare
An accusation or defense.
Renard's discomfort is intense.

He'll suffer whether or not he hangs;
Ysengrin's sharpening his fangs,
Tibert the cat is thinking hard,
And Bruin whose face is red and scarred.
But regardless of their love or hate,
1210   Renard's courage does not abate.
He makes his speech with his head held high,
Looking the king straight in the eye.
    "Sire, I've come to meet you here*
Knowing that you should hold me dear
Above all other lords of this land.
You have been wronged by those who planned
To injure me. Perhaps it's just
My bad luck, but I could never trust
Your love, not for a single day—
1220   That's about as long as I've been away.
You know that there was no ill will
Between us, no dispute, and still,
When I left in peace and by your leave,
You were all ready to believe
Slander about me from my foes.
That is the way a kingdom goes
To ruin—when the king will treat
Without suspicion those who cheat,
And loyalty cannot prevail:
1230   He throws out the head and keeps the tail.
Those who should be serfs by station*
Don't know the wisdom of moderation.
They'll go to any lengths to gain
Favor by someone else's pain.
They'll do evil of any sort
Providing they can rise at court,
Fleecing others as their hearts desire.
And now allow me to inquire
Why Tibert and Bruin complain of me.
1240   Although, should it please Your Majesty,
I can tell you what it's all about.
If I harmed them it was not without

Their help, as they both are well aware.
Who ate the honey if not the bear?
If Lanfroi defends his property,
Should Bruin take it out on me?
Look what he has for legs and paws,
Enormous feet, with enormous claws.
And if Tibert here, my lord the cat,
1250   Was eating a meal of mouse or rat
When he was caught in nets and shamed,
God's heart! I don't see why I am blamed.
As for Ysengrin—what can I say?
His accusation's true, in a way,
For certainly I have loved Hersent.
But that had to be with her consent—
Did she ever come here to protest?
Is it right, at a jealous fool's request,
That I be hanged until I'm dead?
1260   God forbid, Sire! Recognize instead
The good faith and true fidelity*
I have always shown Your Majesty:
Your kingdom, so deserving praise,
Is what I've lived for all my days.
But now my muzzle has gone gray;
There is no game left that I can play,*
By God and Saint George, I'm much too weak.
It's a sin to drag me here to speak,
Old as I am, before this court.
1270   When the king commands that I report,
I do his will, as I hold him dear,
And now I stand in his presence here.
I could hang or perish at the stake;
There is no protest I can make
Against the king—I am not so strong.
But to get revenge that way is wrong.
To hang me will be called a disgrace,
If there's no real judgment on my case."*
"Renard," the emperor begins,
1280   "May your father suffer for his sins!

May the whore who bore you be accursed
Because she didn't abort you first!
Treacherous thief, can you explain
Why you have such a scheming brain?
You know how to argue and to plead,
But to that my court will give no heed.
There's no way for you to leave this place;
You shall hear my verdict on your case!
Your bravado won't be any use;
1290   Your scheming* will find you no excuse.
Though you are as slippery as an eel,
There's no escape and no appeal—
Your fate was predicted long ago,
And now its coming won't be slow.
My noble lords are in court to say
Just what a thief who's caught must pay,
And to sentence a traitor for his crime.
You'll feel the weight of their wrath this time!
Unless you can find a hiding-place,
1300   They'll say what they think right to your face."
Then spoke Grinbert the badger: "Sire,
With the deference that you inspire,*
We give you, and rightly, our full trust.
But that doesn't mean that you can just
Do what you want to—it is vile
To deny a lord his rightful trial.
You may not like it, but it's clear
Renard had safe conduct to come here.
Let those who accuse him state their case,
1310   And then allow him, by your grace,*
With your court as witness, to be tried
As justice and the law provide."
He could not say all he intended.
Before the badger's speech had ended,
Up on his feet was Ysengrin,
And the sheep as well, my lord Belin,
And my lord Tiecelin, the crow,
Chanteclere, Dame Pinte, and also

The three other hens who support their claim.
1320 The hedgehog, Spiky was his name,
And the peacock, Petipas, step out,
And Frobert the cricket—he, no doubt,
Has the loudest voice of those who shout.
Then one with much to complain about:
The squirrel, called my lord Roxat,
And Roenel and Tibert the cat.
Coward the hare, who's very fleet,
Hurries through courtyards, from street to street;
He has very good cause to pray
1330 That justice should be done that day.
Renard is sure if he had to cope
With these he'd have very little hope.
But the king commands that they be still—
Vengeance is subject to his will.
 King Noble's voice, which is very loud,
Carries through the assembled crowd:
"Hear me, my lords," he says in a roar,
"Renard can be trusted like a whore!
What punishment should I decree
1340 To avenge what he has done to me?"
"Sire," they answered, "as you said before,
Renard has the virtue of a whore.
The only thing that's of any use
To reform him is a hangman's noose."
The king replied, "I like what you say!
Let's do it, and without delay!
He's a menace, and I don't know how
We'd get him back if we lost him now.
We'll suffer for it, should he leave:
1350 Some who think they are safe will grieve."
 On a hilltop, by the king's command,
In a rocky place, the gallows stand,
Set up to end the fox's career—
Death, it would seem, is very near.
A monkey, mocking Renard's disgrace,
Is answered by a slap in the face.

Renard looks behind him; he can see
His foes approaching, more than three.
One gives him a kick and one a shove—
He has plenty to be fearful of.
From a good distance—he wouldn't dare
Come any closer—Coward the hare
Did his part too: he threw a stone,
Hit Renard's head, and broke the bone.
But that gave Coward such a fright
That henceforth he stayed out of sight.
One look from Renard put him on edge;
He ran to take shelter in a hedge.
From there, he thought, he could watch and wait
Till Renard had finally met his fate.
But hiding was, I think, a mistake,
He'll have, this day, good cause to shake.
Renard, with stout ropes securing him,
Felt his prospects were growing dim,
He couldn't think of a thing that might
Rescue him from his dreadful plight.
No doubt you'd have to be a master
To walk away from this disaster.
   When he saw the gallows standing there
Renard was reduced to real despair.
He said, "Most gracious lord and king,
Allow me to mention just one thing:

1360

1370

1380

You have had me brought out here and tied,
And want to hang me before I'm tried;
But there are sinful things I've done,
And God's forgiveness could still be won,
Were I allowed, for my soul's defense,
To take the cross in penitence,
And obedient to God's command,

1390   Cross the sea to the Holy Land.
If I die there my soul will rise,
But if I'm hanged I'm the devil's prize—
More honor to you if you relent.
All I want now is to repent."
At the king's feet he lay his head.
Noble was moved by what he'd said.
And then Grinbert came forward to plead
That Renard, repentant, should be freed:
"Before you answer, Sire, think twice!

1400   For God's sake listen to my advice!
Renard's not afraid of any foe.
If he stays away five months you'll know
That your kingdom really can't afford
To lose so fine and valiant a lord."
The king replied, "I'll be more than glad
To lose him, and he'd be twice as bad
Should he return. The best ones trade
Virtue for evil on crusade.
If Renard survives, there is no doubt

1410   That all of us had better look out!"
"If he doesn't get his conscience clear,
Never again will you see him here."
"Then he shall be, by my command,
Forever in the Holy Land."
Renard hears that with a joyful heart.
He may not do any more than start
His journey, so it's no great loss.
On his right shoulder he wears a cross;
They bring him a pilgrim's purse and staff.

1420   Some do not feel inclined to laugh,

Though they kicked and taunted him before;
They fear he will even up the score.
   Behold Renard, ashwood staff in hand,
A pilgrim bound for the Holy Land!
He must forgive them, says the king
In the name of all, for everything;
And if he abandons tricks and lies,
He'll win salvation when he dies.
Whatever Renard may have in mind,
He seems not in the least inclined
To turn away from piety.
He leaves, as he tells His Majesty,*
With peace and forgiveness in his heart;
Just after noon* he's ready to start.
To no else does he say farewell—
He wishes each one of them in Hell!
He'd have revenge on that whole crowd
Except for the king and Fiere the proud,
His courteous and lovely queen
Whose parting words show her far from mean:
"Renard," she says, "we'll pray for you,
And remember us in your prayers too."
"My lady, I will do my best
To show how I honor your request;
And who would not be joyful indeed
To have your prayers in his soul's great need!
But even better would I fare
If I could have that ring you wear.

135

If you allow me that great boon,
1450   You shall be well rewarded soon:
I have jewels* that I will bring
And they're worth a hundred times one ring."
Renard takes the ring that he is handed—
No need for him to be commanded!
Between his teeth he says very low:
"If there is someone who doesn't know
This ring, I have only to appear
For that to cost him very dear."
Renard puts the ring upon his finger,
1460   Bows to the king, and does not linger.
His spurs strike at his horse's sides;
At a racing trot away he rides.
Presently, close at hand, he found
The hedge where Coward went to ground.
It was so long since Renard ate last
He had a headache from his fast.
Coward, seeing Renard so near,
Is just about overcome with fear.
He jumps right up, and in his fright
1470   Greets him, sounding very polite:
"I can hardly tell you what delight
It gives me to see that you're all right!
I have felt weighed down by my dismay
At the way they treated you today."
Replies Renard from his crafty brain,
"If my misfortune gives you pain,
And you see my person so disgraced,
Let's make sure that yours won't go to waste!"
Every word that Coward hears
1480   Seems to justify his gravest fears.
It would be better if he fled
(If he stays he thinks he'll soon be dead*),
And he would have headed for the plain
Had Renard not grabbed his horse's rein.
"Ha! Coward, my lord, by God's heart
I swear you shall not so soon depart!

Did you think your horse had so much speed
That you wouldn't be the one to feed
My hungry cubs at home today?"
1490 With his staff he prods him on his way.
   King Noble, his barons and their men
Were passing through a valley just then
Whose walls towered very high
To four huge rocks set against the sky.
At the top Renard pursues his course
With Coward slung beneath his horse,
Face downward to his bitter shame.
Renard, well deserving his bad name,
Intends, and very soon, to greet
1500 His cubs with a delicious treat.
They'll have Coward for their dinner—
God save him from the crafty sinner!
Renard looks downward through the trees.
There, with the king and queen, he sees
So many beasts and barons swarm*
That the woods are shaking as in a storm.
They talk of Renard, quite unaware
Of what is happening to the hare,
Dragged off, like a convicted thief,
1510 To a prison where he'll come to grief.
Renard tears his cross off, holds it high,
And summons them with a mighty cry:
"My lord king, behold your flag!
I'm giving back the lousy rag!
Those who weighed me down with staff and purse
May God in His own true wisdom curse!"
He wipes himself in a filthy place,
And throws the cross at Noble's face.
Then once again he shouts to the king,
1520 "Listen to me, my lord! I bring
The greetings Noradin* has sent
When I, as a worthy pilgrim, went
To where the pagans across the sea
At the very thought of you will flee."

Renard was so busy having fun
That Coward got his ropes undone,
With a mighty leap was on his horse,
And had set off on a headlong course
Before Renard could realize
1530   That he was about to lose his prize.
Soon Coward, going very fast,
Reached his friends and was safe at last.
His sides had lost quite a lot of skin
Where Renard had stuck his staff right in;
With both his hands and his feet stripped bare—
He really needed a doctor's care.
Just barely able to complete
His journey, he fell at Noble's feet
And told how his life had been at stake.
1540   "Help me, my lord, for God's sweet sake!"
"Oh God, I'm betrayed!" King Noble mourned;
"How utterly is my power scorned!
It's all too easy now to see
How much Renard despises me.
But, my lords, make no mistake—
We know what route Renard will take;
If he makes it home there's not a thing
Can save your necks—you all shall swing!
But whoever captures him shall win
1550   Nobility for all his kin."*
        You should have seen the race begin!
There's Belin the sheep and Ysengrin,
Bruin the bear and Bald the rat,
As well as my lord Tibert the cat.
Dame Pinte and her three good friends appear
And with them, of course, Lord Chanteclere,
Ferran, the horse who carries packs,
Roenel, the watchdog who attacks.
After him comes Frobert the cricket
1560   And then the ferret, Little Sticket,
Followed by the boar Baucent
Whose teeth can make a mighty dent,

138

And of course the raging bull won't lag,
Nor, at a gallop, Bricemer the stag.
The flag is carried by the snail
Who's first in line as they take the trail.
Renard, looking back, can see their haste,
And knows he has little time to waste.
There, first in the field, goes Slow—
1570   The wind is making his banner blow.
What should he do? He can't decide;
Renard jumps out of the path to hide
In the underbrush, and finds a ditch—
But close behind is Short the bitch*
With the others at her heels. They swear
That Renard will never reach his lair,
That their attack will not be stayed
By castle wall or palisade;
The widest moat, the strongest tower,
1580   Thickets, burrows, have no power
To save Renard from the king this time—
On a rope he'll end his life of crime!
Renard feels that his strength has ended.
Flee or go on as he intended,
He knows he'll never reach his home.
His mouth is dripping, white with foam.
And they've very nearly plucked him bare!
Tufts of his robe fly through the air.
His sides are totally abraded—
1590   How can his capture be evaded?
It's a miracle if, nearly in their grip
Renard gives his enemies the slip!
Yet twisting and turning he breaks free,
And is on his way to Maupertuis,
His palace, fortress, mighty tower,
Home and citadel, seat of power,
The one place in all the world he knows
Will keep him safe from his strongest foes.
Let them love or hate him, once he's there
1600   He will wait for them without a care.

His wife embraced him even before
He had a foot inside the door.
Three sons had that noble lady,
One was Malebranche, one Shady,*
The third was named Rovel, and he
Was the handsomest among the three.
They all came running out in haste,
To clasp their arms around his waist,
And seeing his wounds—they were very deep—
1610 Began to comfort him and weep.
They washed his injuries with white wine,
Placed a pillow so that he'd recline;
Then they were ready to serve a meal.
But Renard was too worn out to feel
Like swallowing much of anything
But a chicken leg and half a wing.
He lay in a bath his wife had filled,
And then she bled him. She was skilled
At leechcraft, and before too long
1620 Renard, once again, was feeling strong.

Renard's Pilgrimage

At Maupertuis, his great château,
Renard, a number of years ago,
Was living a very peaceful life.
He wanted no more of endless strife.
He had never given any heed
To the rights of others; in his greed
He'd ruthlessly accumulated
So many things that he was hated
By more men than the year had feasts,
And I think the same was true of beasts.
    But he was changed now, as I say. *
One Friday, early in the day,
Renard emerged from his deep lair,
But not in the way he used to tear
Headlong through the thickest brush—
Now he felt too tired to rush.
"Alas! There is no need anymore
For me to sin as I did before,"
He said. "When I could count on my speed,
I was known for many an evil deed.
In the old days I could run so fast
That I could easily outlast
An army of horsemen on my trail—
They'd chase me all day to no avail,
I only had to dodge a bit.
There was no dog in the land so fit
He could save a chicken I held fast.
God! Have I devoured my last

With so many good hens left to steal?
30 I didn't need a fancy meal
With pepper, garlic or green sauce;
I never even felt the loss
Of wine or beer. I'm a vagabond
And in my travels I was fond
Of stopping wherever I could tell
Capons and hens would likely dwell.
Between my very legs they'd seek
For grain. I'd feel a pecking beak;*
And a bird once firmly in my grip
40 Would make an unexpected trip.
No matter how frantically it cried,
It could only struggle until it died.
Many I've killed that way, I fear.
One I had carried on her bier*
To King Noble's court; she was on display,
An innocent victim of foul play.
From that one I had not a thing—
All they gave me was a chance to swing!
I never acquired by honest means
50 Anything that was worth two beans.
And now I heartily repent
And pray that God omnipotent
Will forgive me all that I've done wrong.
I feel ashamed to have lived so long!"
    Renard's thoughts were none too pleasant.
Suddenly he saw a peasant
Walking along at a steady pace
His hood pulled forward around his face.
The man was alone and Renard, instead
60 Of fleeing, went closer to him and said,
"Hey, peasant! Come over here!
There's no dog with you?" "Have no fear.
You are safe with me," the man replies.
"But Renard, why are there tears in your eyes?"
"Why? Do you really need to be told?
There's not one person, young or old,

In this whole land who would not swear
That I've never travelled anywhere
There was something evil to be done
70   And left before I'd had my fun.
But now I want to change my ways.
I've always heard that if someone prays,
Makes his confession and is shriven,
Whatever his sins, he'll be forgiven."
"Renard, do you really want to confess?"
"I shall without a doubt unless
I can't find the help that I require."
"Renard, you've always been a liar,
A master of deceit and guile.
80   You think I'm a fool! This is just your style."
   "I'm not at all as I was before,
And I promise you what I'm hoping for
Is that you'll help me, by God's grace,
And show me the way to a holy place
And a priest by whom I may be blessed
When all my sins have been confessed."
"Then come with me!" was the man's reply.*
"I was on my way to a church nearby."
   The peasant, being well aware
90   How good a Christian was living there,
Took Renard with him through the wood
To where a hermit's dwelling stood.
A hammer was hanging from a string.
The peasant, knowing how to bring

The priest, gave the door a heavy blow.
The hermit—you could not call him slow—
Came right away to undo the lock.
The sight of Renard gave him a shock.
"*Nomine Mary*! God be praised!

100   Renard, I really am amazed.
What is it brings you to my door?
We've not been so honored here before!"
"Have mercy on me, my lord priest!
I've been a sinner, but now at least
I am here to tell you that I repent.
If you and my other foes consent
To forgive the way that I've behaved,*
It may be that I can still be saved."
Renard knelt in prayer at the hermit's feet.

110   The hermit raised him. "Renard, take this seat
And tell me the evil deeds you've done
Without omitting a single one."
"That, my lord, I'll most gladly do.
Being young and thoughtless, I'd pursue
Innocent hens on whom I dined,
Devouring any I could find
By prowling in hedges where they feed.
I killed them just to content my greed.
With Ysengrin I made a pact,

120   Promising I would always act
In his best interests. And instead,
Not three days after he was wed,
Thanks to me, to the beautiful Hersent,
My sister*, I was not content
Until—to what evil I had sunk!—
I turned him into a cloistered monk,*
And then I had him become a priest.
But when I left him, his joy decreased;
Even a boar's head would have no charm*

130   For Ysengrin, hearing the alarm
I sounded. That required the presence
Of the priest and some two thousand peasants*

Who beat him so when they arrived
The wonder is that he survived.
Then I made him, for my delight,
Fish in a pond one whole long night
Until the next morning when a peasant,
Bludgeon in hand, was most unpleasant.
He and his dog left Ysengrin
140 With not much fur still on his skin
By the time the two of them were done—
And that, I must say, I thought great fun.
After that I caught him in a snare,
And for a week he stayed right there.
He escaped, but his foot remained behind—
God! How my sins weigh on my mind!
Madame Hersent had to have her share.
I tied her to the tail of a mare
Which I bit so it would kick and buck,
150 And left Hersent to try her luck.
I've played so many tricks like these,
Committed such frauds and felonies,
I'm sure I've been excommunicated.
Even if all day long you waited,
I couldn't tell half my sins, God knows,
But they're all like these. If you impose
Fit penance, that's my only hope."
"Renard, you'll have to talk to the Pope
In Rome. You can't be helped unless
160 You go there and truthfully confess.
That is the penance that you need."
Renard said, "That is penance indeed."
    "And he commits a further crime
Who knows what to do and then wastes time."
    Renard sees now that he must obey.
With staff in hand he is on his way,
His long journey has begun.
He acts like a pilgrim and looks like one.
Around his neck hangs a handsome purse.
170 But he thinks it foolish to fare worse

Than he has to. If he must atone,
There's no need for doing it all alone.*
He left the main road to Rome behind,
And took the first path he could find
To the left, which presently revealed,
As he followed it across a field,
A giant flock of grazing sheep,
Among them Sir Belin, half-asleep.
His service was so much in demand
180   That now the poor beast could hardly stand.
"What are you doing?" Renard said.
"I'm resting because I feel half dead."
"But Belin, you know it's wrong to shirk."*
The ram said, "I cannot do more work.
The foul peasant for whom I slave
Refuses me the rest I crave.
Ever since the day I found my voice
I've covered his ewes. I had no choice.
The flock you see before your eyes
190   Is the product of my enterprise.
And now I've discovered that my lord
Will give me an ill-deserved reward:
Those who sow his fields will have my meat
For pay, and my skin will warm the feet
Of someone who has no boots at home
And wants to make a trip to Rome."
"To Rome!" said Renard, "if that is so,
By God, it's no way for you to go!
Better your skin with you inside
200   Than for it to travel when you have died.
To escape that fate won't help in the least,
For just after Easter there's the feast
Of Rogation* pious people keep
On a Thursday when they dine on sheep.
It's clear to me you're as good as dead
If you don't get out of here instead,
And I think you had better not delay."
"Renard, by the Lord to whom we pray

(You are a pilgrim, as I see),
210 Can I believe what you counsel me?"
"Strange as it may no doubt appear,
My pilgrimage is not insincere.
I know I've earned an evil name,
But now I've reformed, and my whole aim
Is to carry out as best I can
The instruction of a pious man
So that I, with the help of God, can win
Forgiveness for my life of sin.
God's command makes it very clear
220 We must give up all that we hold dear
To serve him: family, land, and grass.*
Our life in this world will quickly pass,
And all of us are condemned to woe
Unless we change our ways. We know
That God is happier when he sees
One repentant sinner on his knees
Than ninety-nine who need not beg.
This whole world isn't worth an egg.
That is why I'm about to leave
230 For Rome where I'm hoping to receive
Advice from the Pope that will keep me straight.
If you come with me, you'll avoid the fate
Of having your skin cut up to suit
The fit of someone else's boot."
"A pilgrim's advice one must obey,"
Said Belin. "I'm with you all the way!"
   And so the two of them departed.
Not long after their journey started,
They met a high priest* both of them knew,
240 Grazing in a ditch where thistles grew.
"Bernard, God save you!" Renard said.
The high priest, startled, raised his head.
"God's blessing on you, too," said he
"Is that Renard the fox* I see?"
"Yes indeed, my good Sir, it is I."
"What scheme, I wonder, is the reason why

You've equipped yourselves as pilgrims do,
For Belin, it seems, is in it too!"
"There isn't any scheme at all.
250   Both of us simply heard the call,
And God's forgiveness is what we'll gain
By gladly enduring toil and pain.
But to this you clearly don't aspire,
Nor to pilgrimage. Your heart's desire
Is to carry all year long a stack
Of heavy logs upon your back,
Or under sacks of coal to stoop
While a pointed stick plays on your croup
Until there's not one unbroken spot.
260   And then in summer when it's hot,
A multitude of flies invade
Even the places where there's shade.
Come with us. You'll be doing what's right,
And then, no matter what your plight,
There'll be two of us to help you out,
And food enough to keep you stout."
The donkey replied, "I'll be very glad
To join you, if there's food to be had."
Renard said, "That I can guarantee."
270   So now the pilgrims number three.*

        In a place where the woods were very thick,
It seemed that they could have their pick
Of roe deer and does and even stags,
But they didn't manage to fill their bags.
In all the forest they didn't find
A farm or dwelling of any kind,*
Far as they travelled that first day.
"Where can we find a place to stay?"
Said Belin, "Soon it will be night."
280   His lordship Bernard said, "Belin's right."
"My dear companions," Renard replied,
"Why do we need to sleep inside?
I'd choose the soft grass beneath this tree
Before a palace, were it up to me."

"By my faith, Renard," said Belin the sheep,
"I'd rather a house in which to sleep!
Out here we're likely to be attacked
By three or four wolves; I know for a fact
These woods are home for more than a few."
290   And to this the high priest said, "That's true."
Renard answered with no show of pride,
"I'll go along with what you decide.
For lodging I suggest we try
My kinsman's* place; he lives close by,
And we can depend on him. Let's go!
He'll be glad to welcome us, I know."
The others do not hesitate
And are soon inside. But a dreadful fate
Will come upon them before they leave,
300   If Renard can't pull a trick from his sleeve
That can rescue them. The wolf and Hersent
Were galloping through the woods, intent
On finding something on which to dine.
The pilgrims found their lodgings fine,
Provided with bread and cheese, salt meat—
Just what pilgrims would want to eat—
And a plentiful supply of beer.
Belin drank so much that in his good cheer
He began to sing with all his heart,
310   The high priest took up the basso's part
And Renard's falsetto made the third.
Too bad that they were overheard
As their peaceful song filled the wolf's abode!
Ysengrin came back with a heavy load
He was carrying between his jaws.
Hersent, quite frantic, and for good cause—
She felt just about to die of thirst—
Was right beside him when they first
Heard strange music come from within.
320   They paused as their ears filled with the din.
The wolf said, "There is someone inside."
"I'll go and see," Hersent replied,

And putting her burden on the ground
She looked through a hole in the wall* and found
The pilgrims gathered around the fire.
More than that she did not require,
But turned away to describe the sight
To Ysengrin: "We're in luck tonight!
The donkey, Belin, and Renard are there
330   As if we had caught them in a snare."
They banged on the door with all their might
But nothing happened: it stayed closed tight.
"Open the door! Open up at once!"
"Be quiet! Do you take me for a dunce?"
"Renard, don't you tell me to be quiet!
You can't keep me out, and don't try it!
Foul traitor, for this day I've waited
Ever since my foot was amputated.
Open up! There's no way you'll contrive
340   To get yourself out of here alive!
That goes for the sheep and the donkey too."
"Alas!" said Belin. "What shall we do?
We'll all be killed!" "Don't be upset,"
Said Renard, "they haven't killed us yet.
If you want to get out of this, you can—
Just go along with my little plan."
Bernard said, "Your skills I do not doubt.
You brought us here and you'll get us out.
We'll gladly follow where you lead."
350   "Sir Bernard, you have the strength we need.

Against this door if you'll put your back,
We can let it open just a crack
And the wolf will think that we've complied.
As soon as he gets his head inside,
You give a shove, the door will slam
And the wolf will joust with our friend the ram."
Behind the door Bernard was hidden,
Leaving it open as he was bidden.
Ysengrin's neck was caught in the trap
360   When the door closed tight with a wicked snap:
Where he was captured, he would stay.
If only you could have seen the way
The ram proceeded to do his part,
Backing up for a running start
And butting to Renard's refrain:
"Come on, Belin! Let's see his brain!
Stop when you've killed him, not before!"
Not in all the world, at any door,
Has there been such a fierce and bloody show,
370   As Belin struck blow after heavy blow
With his great horns. He would not quit
Until poor Ysengrin's skull was split.
   Hersent was unable to get through
To help him. All that she could do
Was gallop her fastest through the wood,
Howling as loudly as she could
To summon all the wolves she found—
A hundred or more. Then she turned around
And came charging back to avenge her mate.
380   The three had decided not to wait,
But clear tracks showed the way they'd fled,
And the wolves followed them. (Hersent led,
Promising vengeance.) They were beaten.
The wolves swore they would soon be eaten.
Their bodies no one would ever find.
Renard heard them howling close behind
And urged on his friends, "Let's get out of here!"
The high priest, farting in his fear,

Had never learned how to put on speed;
390 Renard understands that now indeed
He must think up a ruse if he intends
To save them. "What shall we do, my friends?
We are all dead, it seems to me.
Let's hide in the branches of this tree.
That way we'll throw them off our track.
You know how Hersent would pay us back
For what we did to her lord back there."
Belin the ram said, "I don't care!
I've never climbed, and I can't start now."
400 The high priest said, "I don't know how."
"Believe me, my lords, in times of need
It's wonderful how you can succeed
In doing something you'd never try
Except when it's either that or die.
Come on, my good lords, climb! climb!
Save yourselves while you still have time!"
Renard climbed up and, hard-pressed,
His two companions did their best
Until, with a scramble and a lurch,
410 Each of them somehow found a perch.
    And here comes Hersent, not sparing the spurs,
Close followed by those friends of hers.
But by the time they had reached that place,
They couldn't see the slightest trace
Of their quarry. They looked all around
And decided their prey had gone to ground.
So they all stretched out wearily,
Right where they were, beneath the tree.
Lord Belin had a terrible fright—
420 And no wonder—when he saw that sight.
"Alas, if I could only choose,
I'd be home right now among my ewes!"
Bernard said, "I'm all stiff and sore.
I was never so poorly lodged before—
I absolutely have to move!"
Renard was quick to disapprove:

"Soon enough we'll hear you curse
When you find you've moved from bad to worse!"
Bernard said, "I intend to try."
430   And Belin said, "Then so do I."
Renard said, "Why reason with a dunce?"
His two companions moved at once,
And, hanging on for all they were worth
As they lost their balance, fell to earth.
Four wolves were squashed* beneath Bernard,
Belin killed two, he fell so hard.
At the sight of their companions dead,
The other wolves in terror fled
In all directions. Seeing them routed,
440   Renard, from his lookout, shouted,
"After them, my beauties! Tally ho!
Hang on, Belin! Bernard, let's go!
Sink your teeth in, my brave high priest!"
At that the speed of the wolves increased,
And for fifty silver marks Hersent,
If asked to turn back, would not consent.
   After Renard had watched them flee,
He joined his friends beneath the tree.
"Tell me, my lords, are you all right?
450   Our enemies are out of sight,
And I've saved you from a dreadful fate."
Bernard said, "I'm in such a state

153

I certainly can't go on to Rome—
I only hope I can get back home."
Belin said, "That's where I'm going too.
I'll leave the pilgrimage to you."
Renard said, "On my head I swear
This travelling is a sad affair.
Visits to Rome were not required

460 Of many whose virtue is admired;
Worthy pilgrims, on the other hand,
May turn to sin in the Holy Land.
I'm going home, since no one needs
A pilgrimage to do good deeds,
Content to earn an honest living
So that I can help the poor by giving."
"Onward Christian soldiers!"* they shout.
That's how their pilgrimage turned out.

Notes

INTRODUCTION

1. Lucien Foulet, *Le Roman de Renard*, Librairie Honoré Champion, Paris, 1968, p. 498. I have followed Foulet's chronology in all references to the dating of the various branches.

2. Foulet (pp. 165–189) has convincingly demonstrated the unity of Branches II and Va. The title given to the two branches together in this translation is "Renard and Ysengrin the Wolf."

3. The beginning of Branch I refers to "Perrot," the rest of whose name was contributed by the author of Branch XVI.

4. Robert Bossuat, *Le Roman de Renard*, Hatier, Paris, 1967, p. 180.

5. R. Howard Bloch, *Medieval French Literature and Law*, University of California Press, 1977, p. 114. Louis VII's truce lasted for ten years beginning in 1155, some twenty years before the writing of these poems. Otherwise the ability to impose a universal peace—that is, to divert all aggression to their own wars—was a dream of kings rather than a reality.

6. Jean Graven, *Le Procès criminel du Roman de Renart*, Georg & Cie., Genève, 1950, p. 35.

7. Foulet (p. 203, n. 2) may be justified in minimizing this reaction, but at least it reflects, with implicit irony, the king's prejudice in favor of Renard.

8. Graven, pp. 26–27.

9. C. S. Lewis, *The Discarded Image*, Cambridge University Press, London, 1970, p. 205.

10. Kenneth Varty's recent work (*Nottingham Medieval Studies*. XXIX. 1985) persuasively opposes Foulet's views concerning authorship of these *branches*. I am obliged to Brian Levy for the reference.

BRANCH II

Line 1. The translation is based on the Martin edition as reprinted in 1970 by Dufournet with the corrections suggested by Martin and by Gunnar Tilander. Major differences between this and the other reliable edition, that of Cangé, which I refer to as C, are noted.

The designation *branche* occurs in the *Roman de Renart* itself; Tilander notes it in Branch IV, line 19; Branch VII, line 193; and Branch IX, line 5 (Gunnar Tilander, *Lexique du Roman de Renart*, Librairie Honoré Champion, Paris, 1971).

Line 6. La Chievre's *Tristan* is unknown to us, but it is interesting that Pierre de Saint-Cloud mentions a version of the poem, since Ysengrin occasionally resembles King Mark, and Hersent, Iseut.

Line 10. *Yvain (Le Chevalier au Lion)*, Chrétien de Troyes.

Line 19. *Barons* is understood here and throughout the text to mean simply lords, or vassals.

Line 22. As Foulet points out (p. 174), Branch II is not really concerned with the war itself but rather relates its beginning. The *desfiance* mentioned in this line is the formal declaration which, provided it is properly communicated to the opponent, allows one to kill someone without incurring the penalties attached to murder.

Line 26. "Farm" translates *vile*, which may also mean "village."

Line 28. C has line 28 as in Martin, followed by Martin's XXIV, lines 1–42, and then continues with Martin's 23ff.

Line 41. C adds the indispensable beehives.

Line 52. The changes of tense from past to present which occur so frequently in medieval poetry are to some extent imitated in the translation.

Lines 114–119. In C, Chanteclere is nervous, but he still behaves in accordance with his words.

Line 254. Adopting the variant *nos nos retornerons* (Foulet, p. 414).

Line 279. C has Renard also take a nap, using a stone for a pillow, while he waits to be sure of Chanteclere.

Line 307. *cosins germeins.*

Line 309. He sang a *sonet*, a song.

Lines 353–368. This passage has no equivalent in C.

Line 368. Foulet (p. 167) comments on Pinte's transformation into a great lady whose lamentations might be those of a heroine of epic.

Line 413. The text specifies that Malvoisin (bad neighbor) is the name of Constant's dog. In the various passages involving lists of names, the translation sometimes attempts to suggest the meaning of the name, sometimes gives a free adaptation, or keeps the original, prompted by considerations of sound and rhythm.

Line 414. Renard le ros.

Line 475. The titmouse is a *conmere* of Renard's. Their exact relationship is unclear except that Renard had served as godfather to the bird's son. The universal peace Renard speaks of is considered by Foulet (p. 179) to be an invention of Renard which becomes true later on within the fiction. However, King Noble's references to this truce seem rather to originate in his own jurisdiction, misused though it may be by such vassals as Renard.

Line 505. Using Tilander's explanation that *flatter* means "deceive" rather than "compliment."

Line 520. plein le poing.

Line 603. A *convers.* Foulet points out (pp. 156–157) that both this episode and the following encounter with Tibert were invented by Pierre de Saint-Cloud.

Lines 669–671. C does not include the attractive playfulness of the cat.

Line 702. As C has it, Ysengrin is Tibert's *conpere.*

Line 805. vielz est li chaz.

Line 843. C breaks off here and goes on to Martin's Branch XV, lines 1–46.

Line 867. solleillier.

Lines 870–871. The slight awkwardness of these lines was perhaps intended to suggest Tiecelin's cautious observations. When it comes to diving on the cheese, the expression is *laisse corre,* familiar from those moments in epic when a hero gallops straight toward an opponent.

Line 888. mes barbes roro.

Line 893. de cuit en eve et de rosti.

Line 899. Renard and the crow are said to be *ajorné,* "summoned," in the judicial sense.

Line 928. A *rotruenge.*

Line 938. Tilander (*Lexique,* p. 110) quotes an apparently knowledgeable source to the effect that eating nuts has been from ancient times considered harmful to the vocal cords.

Line 1012. del nostre.

Line 1020. poison, originally simply a beverage, later medicinal and/or poisonous.

Line 1038. Ysengrin is *connestable*, in principle a military position. In Branch Va, line 292, however, he is said to be *connestable* of the king's house and of his table, a position which would be more like that of a seneschal.

Line 1043. *sale*, a nice junction of lair and château.

Line 1050. I have been unable to find an explanation for this line except for Professor Joan Ferrante's suggestion to me that it might have something to do with the head covering that distinguishes married from unmarried ladies in medieval songs. In that case, Hersent, although obviously a matron, would be showing her inclination to unmatronly behavior.

Line 1089. Renard's inspired, and fictional, explanation of his apparent neglect of Hersent was certainly adequate for its immediate purpose of turning her irritation toward her husband. We don't know how much else he might have hoped to accomplish by it, but the event would seem to have surpassed his calculations. As noted in the Introduction, Hersent is vastly transformed from her irreproachable model in *Ysengrimus*.

Line 1124. *si comme il erent arrengié*. This phrase would certainly indicate that Hersent was a conspirator in the attack on her cubs, which seems most unlikely. It is true, however, that she had no particular objections. The anger of the cubs is indispensable to the plot, because once Hersent was welcoming to Renard there would be no other way to inform Ysengrin of her infidelity, particularly in such a way as not to leave room for any doubt.

Line 1189. Ysengrin's speech alternates between vulgar abuse and a more elegant diction, just as his reaction to the evidence is influenced by his anger or by his hopes that Hersent is after all innocent. In both aspects he resembles Beroul's King Mark.

Line 1210. Foulet (pp. 172–173) indicates these lines as the formal *desfiance* of Ysengrin to Renard, the true beginning of the war. It is clear, however, that there is no way for Renard to have been aware of it.

Line 1217. *une aventure estrange*.

Line 1218. Tilander's interpretation.

Line 1250. This is apparently Maupertuis. Renard's home is called Mailcrues in C as well (Branch VIIb, line 6766).

Line 1259. *chastiaux*.

Line 1261. *tasniere*.

Line 1263. Renard's den clearly had more than one entrance.

Line 1279. *ses iex voyantz* is obviously not to be taken literally as it is in line 1361.

Line 1282. *c'est force et force soit.*

Lines 1287–1290. These remarks, which Renard attributes to Hersent, have no apparent reference to the earlier scene of Renard's visit to her. Foulet (p. 143) suggests that the passage may be related to Marie de France's fable on the subject.

Line 1314. *Ne draps levez ne braie traite.*

Lines 1351–1352. A. M. Schmidt's interpretation, cited by Dufournet.

Line 1392. Following Foulet's indications, the last four lines of Branch II have been omitted:

> He knows that Renard, without a care,
> Is safe from vengeance, deep in his lair,
> So Ysengrin goes back to his own,
> To his household underneath the stone.

The translation continues with Branch Va, line 257.

BRANCH Va

Line 257. Ysengrin, having rescued Hersent, suffers a violent and characteristic change of mood. The C manuscript continues directly from the moment Hersent is dragged out by her tail: *Quand Isangrin la vit delivre: / Hai! fait il, pute orde livre.*

Line 281. The duel is replaced in Branch Va by an oath. A later author relates the judicial combat (Branch VI). Ysengrin won, but Renard was saved from the resulting death sentence by the intervention of a priest.

Graven (p. 30) points out that Saint Louis, in an ordinance of 1260, required that court cases be decided by hearing witnesses rather than by single combat.

Line 298. See note to Branch II, line 1038.

Line 301. *La cour estoit granz et plenere.*

Line 302. *Bestes i ot.* But it is in this part of the narrative that the animals leave their woods and farms to become, almost completely, Noble's aristocratic vassals. Ysengrin himself, for example, only recently tracking Renard, nose to the ground, "speaks several languages."

Line 329. Renard ne dote mariage / Ne parenté ne cosinnage;

Line 366. chevela.

Line 371. Ysengrin, having believed Hersent's version of Renard's visit, is concerned only about the subsequent rape. This was in any case a far more serious charge than simple adultery and was punishable by death (Foulet, p. 198; also Graven, pp. 39–40).

Line 405. Mes sires, qui bien est estables.

Line 431. The king's argument is rather like Renard's when he said he was trying to help Hersent by pushing her, difficult to dispute and wholly unconvincing. Noble, of course, is prejudiced in Renard's favor and totally neglects the charge of rape.

The king's role, in any case, was limited to listening to the accusation, summoning the accused, and handing the case over to his council for a decision (Graven, p. 22).

Line 457. Foulet (pp. 219–223) identifies the Lombard camel as the papal legate Pierre de Pavie, whose Italian accent and Latin legal jargon must have been conspicuous. The translation attempts to imitate the text's mangled Latin mixed with Italian and French. The camel's language is only clear enough to let the basic message come through: justice should be the primary concern of a king.

Line 498. Like Charlemagne in *La Chanson de Roland*, King Noble customarily listens with his head down (cf. line 388).

Line 499. The king addresses himself to *vos qui ci estes / Li plus vaillant, les granor bestes,* but it is not clear whether he refers to his vassals in general, as opposed, perhaps, to those of other kings, or is making a requirement for members of the council. In any case the council, of vast size, includes the deer as a significant speaker, but the barnyard animals do not appear.

Line 504. Foulet (p. 200) says this is an interesting question: "Si Hersent est innocente, Renard peut-il être coupable?" His suggestion is that Noble implies that Hersent is precisely *not* innocent. But either way the charge of rape should stand.

Line 506. tref roial.

Line 511. Bricemer's personal attitude toward Ysengrin makes his concern for fair evidence particularly impressive. Baucent is also commendable in this respect.

Line 519. asemblé sont au parlement.

Line 579. The fact that Plateaux recalls that Renard robbed Ysengrin is one of the links between Branches II and Va, because the episode is related nowhere else (Foulet, pp. 187–188).

Line 595.   borse trouvée. According to Gunnar Tilander (*Remarques sur le Roman de Renart*, Elanders Boktryckeri Aktiebolag, Göteborg, 1923, p. 70), this expression, although traceable to tales of unexpected riches, simply means to be very happy.

Lines 601–602.   Tilander (*Remarques*, p. 70) cites proverbs analogous to the first (*a tel morsel itel tece*) and says that the second is frequently found as it stands (*Chaz set bien qui barbes il leche*), and in various languages.

Line 606.   That is, the king favors Renard and laughs at Ysengrin.

Line 654.   The cabbage leaves must have been enormous to hide a bear!

Line 664.   All crowds in the *Roman* are of improbable size, as in epic. In C there are seven thousand peasants in this group.

Line 678.   besoing fet vielle troter.

Line 684.   peliçon.

Line 699.   A very familiar epic formula—Bruin sees himself as a kind of Roland.

Line 751.   Bruin is not initiating a judicial procedure, which depends on a formal complaint, a *clame.*

Line 755.   Bruin seems to forget that Tiecelin's feathers were scarcely the prize Renard was after.

Line 768.   Baucent may not be quite as long-winded as Bruin, but his style is heavy, as he is, and he tends to repeat himself.

Line 794.   The translation reflects Foulet's suggestion that Cointereau's obscure speech is clarified in lines 863–867.

Line 824.   meins et piez.

Lines 843–854.   This speech is attributed to Cointereau in C, and it does indeed sound more like him.

Line 849.   This line refers to various proverbs suggesting that the size of wolves always grows in the description (Tilander, *Remarques*, p. 77).

Line 850.   This proverb exists in the opposite sense: *Et granz vens ciet de poi de pluie* (loc. cit.).

Line 872.   Foulet (p. 203, pp. 223–225) suggests that Bricemer may be referring to an absence already expected, perhaps in connection with the papal legate's visit which, if Pierre de Pavie is the model, would have had to do with a crusade. The king's enthusiasm for the council's decision appears to reflect his disinclination to participate in the proceedings, but Foulet may well be right in seeing in his reaction primarily relief that a decision has been taken which is so likely to favor Renard.

Line 873. Another example of Bricemer's tendency to give bad advice with the best of intentions.

Line 934. This would seem already to have been done.

Line 942. C has *vostre part,* the decision being the council's and not the king's.

Line 962. Failure to obey a court summons was equivalent to an admission of guilt, and the penalty could be hanging. Usually a certain number of court sessions, often three, could go by before the absentee was formally considered in default (Graven, p. 27). In Branch I, Renard, much more seriously threatened since the king had already decided to hang him, nevertheless goes to court when the third messenger arrives with the king's formal summons.

Line 972. Three days before, in C.

Line 976. Roenel's reaction is purely canine, but the truce offered is a private one, as between barons.

Line 994. C is more specific: *Que vos saiez dou plest a mi / tant que nos l'aions confondu.*

Line 1033. In the case of a *serment purgatoire,* the accused is accompanied by his *co-jureurs* (Graven, p. 28). The number of them, and the importance given to their presence, indicates how closely the possibility of a recourse to violence was felt to underlie a procedure so dependent on good faith.

Line 1040. The detail of description makes us see the stag once again.

Lines 1042–1043. Presumably the Lombard camel. The name is pejorative and means one who wastes his time on idle matters.

Line 1056. In C these are the only ones who swear fidelity to Ysengrin.

Line 1068. Those who carry the battle flags are subject to particular mockery. The army chasing Renard in Branch I is led by Slow the Snail.

Line 1070. See note to Branch I, line 472.

Line 1089. After line 1089, C has three lines about *li connins,* who didn't come because he was frightened, but with whom Renard has a truce. This doesn't make much sense and repeats the rhyme *s'eschive / trive,* which applied to Roenel's meeting with Ysengrin; but this rabbit may have become the unfortunate Coward the hare of Branch I.

Line 1098.   C has simply two groups of allies, Ysengrin's on the plain and Renard's on the mountainside.

Line 1127.   *Seint Roënau le rechingnié.*

Line 1132.   *se recorce et se brace.*

Line 1146.   At this point C diverges completely from Martin. Renard's speech turns to thoughts of food, and eventually he traps Bruin into still another search for honey, Tibert with him (to the great discomfort of both), while Renard makes off with a goose and mocks his victims from the safety of Maupertuis.

Line 1180.   One feels that Renard would not have hesitated to perjure himself, but in fact he doesn't. Foulet's remark on the subject is worth quoting: "L'intérêt que montre l'auteur pour tout ce qui est légal, ne va pas sans une secrète admiration des formes et des procédés de la justice sociale. L'auteur est une manière de légiste en gaîté qui caricature sans amertume des institutions qu'au fond il respecte" (Foulet, p. 207).

Line 1186.   *lance levee sor le fautre.*

Lines 1200ff.   Here, as in Branch I, lines 665ff., a number of the names recall the heroes of epic.

Line 1254.   As Renard said to Bruin in line 678.

Lines 1257–1258.   The author, perhaps getting out of breath, gives three names for four dogs.

B R A N C H   I

Line 3.   The primary intention of *son cher conpere* here would seem to be ironic, but Renard and Ysengrin are often said to be cousins (Branch Va, line 328) and at one point enter into a formal familial alliance, emphasized more in the late-twelfth-century *Reinhart Fuchs* than in the *Roman* (Foulet, p. 430).

Line 11.   This *estoire* is not Pierre de Saint-Cloud's poem, but the anonymous authority to which medieval writers like to refer. Here the author seems to parody the tradition, as he does in his evocation to spring in the following lines.

Lines 15–18.   Major convocations of vassals at the king's court coincided with major holy days or important secular events. King Arthur's court in the springtime provides a setting for various romances, and in *Le Chevalier de la charette* Chrétien places it specifically during the Feast of the Ascension. King Arthur and King Noble have, in any case, much in common, including wives who do not entirely conform to their royal dignity.

Line 34. This version of the story places the rape in the den rather than at the entrance to Maupertuis. Of course, having read Branch II, the author would be under no illusions as to Hersent's actual conduct. On the other hand, if the "real" attack on Hersent is forgotten while Hersent's story remains unconvincing, Renard's character is more attractive in Branch I than in the earlier narrative.

Line 41. "He was warned" would have revealed, to a careful listener, Ysengrin's complicity in the substitution of a dangerous dog for the relics on which Renard was to swear (Branch Va, lines 980–1154).

Line 50. Foulet (p. 343) sees here a possible allusion to the conjugal life of Eleanor of Aquitaine.

Lines 55–78. The bear is characteristically poised between the simplistic and the fundamental. He would be quite unaware that there is anything comical in his expression of feudal obligation (line 68). On the other hand, his great size lets him undertake his mission to Renard with a confidence others will not show.

Lines 62–63. See note 5 to the Introduction.

Line 74. Graven (p. 49) points out that compensation was due to the seigneur as well as to the victim because crime is a breaking of the peace.

Line 79. Clamor does not appear in Branches II or Va.

Lines 99–102. The bull is too carried away to notice how accusing Hersent weakens his attack on Renard.

Line 102. *Vos monta onques es arçons.*

Line 103. The badger is Renard's cousin and his only real defender, although he is too intelligent not to approach the fox with caution and due suspicion. He agrees to be an envoy to Renard only if he is given an official letter with the king's seal; he arrives nervously at Maupertuis, where he is greeted by Renard with genuine hospitality, and waits until the end of the meal before revealing his mission, a prudence the author calls to our attention (lines 971–973).

Lines 109–110. This is an important point, because breaking and entering was a hanging matter (Graven, pp. 43–44). These lines have no equivalent in C.

Lines 120–121. It is at least certain that Renard stole Ysengrin's provisions, and Grinbert, a wise lawyer, directs attention to this relatively innocuous guilt. However, this passage may mean simply that if anything at all is owed to Ysengrin, he will be repaid after the trial.

Lines 132–133. The masculine pronouns would seem to refer to Renard. Ysengrin would be unlikely to call his wife, estranged or not, *belle soeur,* and certainly would not "fear" her. Grinbert has just finished justifying the adultery as far as Renard is concerned, but now maintains that Hersent deserves to be "fried like bacon" if she persists.

Line 135. For this line alone the author of Branch I would deserve to be considered the most skillful of writers presenting animals in human guise. He never reminds us of their identity until we have forgotten it, but we never forget it for long, and he, unlike the authors of the less successful branches, never does.

Lines 136–178. Hersent recalls Iseut by the dramatic eloquence of her speech, her offer to submit to an ordeal, her tone of despairing innocence, and particularly by her way of admitting her guilt while seeming most emphatically to deny it (lines 149–150, 177–178).

Line 159. Foulet (p. 108) quotes Martin's observation that Easter fell on April 1 in 1179 and in 1184, the former being the probable date of Branch I.

Line 188. On the subject of conjugal infidelity, the medieval poet cannot resist having the donkey complain of women, even if it diminishes his credibility as a beast. This does not occur in C, which has *Dame Hersent* in the place of *totes femes.*

Line 191. Here the real donkey reappears. Foulet has called attention to the charm of this line.

Lines 201–206. C uses similar words but clearly intends to vituperate rather than sympathize with Renard because no one will believe him. These lines in Martin read in favor of Renard except for the word *forsenes,* "out of one's senses," translated here as "wild." After line 206, C inserts several lines accusing Renard of having heard about but ignoring the offer Hersent has in fact just made of trial by ordeal, concluding with an enigmatic remark about how everyone gangs up on a defenseless person, presumably Hersent. Following this it is Grinbert who appeals to the king for clemency and offers to fetch Renard.

Lines 219–227. It is uncertain whether the council considered Renard to be guilty of a felony, in which case he is not to be summoned but forced to appear, or whether he is guilty only of having not

yet responded to the king's general summons. The latter would
seem more likely in view of the suggestion that they wait two more
days. In any event, one of the major judicial problems of the age
was how to coerce accused persons into appearing in court (Bloch,
p. 65). The role of King Noble as judge is similar to that of Charlemagne in *La Chanson de Roland* (and, like him, Noble is called
emperor as well as king). He makes the ultimate decisions, but only
in accordance with the majority opinion of his assembled vassals,
as Charlemagne could not condemn Ganelon out of his own con-
victions. The king could more readily make negative judgments.
Charlemagne refused advice that was not to his liking, such as
sending one of the seven peers as envoy to Marsile. Similarly, Noble
refuses to allow Renard to be condemned *in absentia*, whether for
contempt of court or for a felony. Later he is disposed to condemn
Renard without more proof than the body of a mangled hen, he
vows an exemplary vengeance, and the written message he sends
to Renard condemns him to be hanged. There is no doubt, however,
that this verdict would have been fully approved by the vast majority
of the vassals. Renard comes to court in the face of this sentence,
because not to do so would be to plead guilty both to failing to
attend the court without cause in the first place and to the felonies
which so aroused the king's wrath. When he appears it is in a spirit
of righteous indignation, heroic acting under the circumstances.

Line 229. forsjugier; to arrive at a verdict "outside," without
proper judicial proceedings.

Line 230. C has *Tout ce poons nos bien laissier,* that is, "we really
needn't discuss this any further," in place of the recourse to superior
military strength, so characteristic of irritated warlords, in Martin.
Both versions emphasize Noble's preference for Renard, which seems
to be based on an affectionate enjoyment of his unscrupulous cleverness rather than on self-interest, although Renard will claim,
apparently justifiably, to be the most valuable of Noble's vassals
(lines 1212–1215), somewhat in the style of Roland's boasting to
Charlemagne.

Line 240. C has Ysengrin saying he will accept the ordeal if the
king wishes, followed directly by his objections.

Lines 240–246. Ysengrin's unpleasant egocentricity, his lack of
confidence in Hersent, or in trial by ordeal, are simultaneously
shown here. Again the appeal is to force, this time frustrated by
the king's peace, but only as a second argument, the first being that
Renard is in fact the stronger, if only by superior cunning.

Line 272. Cf. Hersent's fur in line 136.

Line 283. Literally: "now the fire is difficult to put out."

Line 286. As with saints, it seems reasonable to assume that names chosen at random will be convenient for the rhyme, and that a translator may, with discretion, proceed similarly. Hence *la Rossete* becomes "Roseanne."

Line 295. C (line 311) reads "When the king had eaten enough" rather than judged enough.

Line 298. *paumes battant.*

Lines 301–337. The tone and vocabulary of the speech alternate between the nobly dramatic (*conseilliez ceste chaitive! Mort, car me pren . . .*) and those appropriate to a hen. At some moments the two levels of meaning coincide to wonderful effect, as in lines 320–321 when "plump" (*crasse*) reminds us that in this context its meaning, and that of "tender" as well, would have to convey the idea of "edible."

Line 302. The fact that Pinte specifically appeals to the dog and wolf underscores the most profound irony in the poem. Of all the beasts present they are the most likely to dine off a plump hen and, regardless of peace treaties, cannot do otherwise. Perhaps the rather obscure phrase *tex con vox estes* (literally: "such as you are"), which otherwise looks like mere filler, is meant to contribute to this suggestion. The phrase in C, *si con vos estes* (roughly, "all those who are here") does not.

Line 313. Gonbert del Frenne is the farmer who owned the hens.

Line 314. In C the repetition of *angroissoit / angrissa* ("to fatten") seems more convincing than Martin's *pussoit* ("he fed") / *anguissoit*, since a farmer raising hens would be unlikely to "torment" or "harass" them to lay eggs.

Line 328. *pelices.*

Lines 339–340. Fainting is common in romance, group fainting in epic (100,000 men at one point in *La Chanson de Roland*). Again it is the dog and wolf who are especially helpful. Without proper names, however, the author may not mean Ysengrin and Roenel.

Line 346. That the hens address themselves to King Noble is only to be expected, but the "documentation" makes both their gesture and itself humorous.

Line 352. *baceler:* an aspiring knight and thus, perhaps, more interesting to the king than are mere hens, or ladies (unless Chanteclere's woe, being more restrained, was even more impressive than theirs).

Line 360. The cure of Coward's fever will make Renard's crime the more heinous by sanctifying his victim. Few medieval narratives are as tightly organized as is Branch I.

Line 371. C specifies that retribution must wait until after the funeral.

Line 392. foreins.

Line 393. Noble, perhaps prompted by Ysengrin's applause, returns to the accusation of adultery and now supports it.

Line 399. In C Noble himself apparently hands Bruin the stole (*Prenez ceste estole*) and asks Clamor to commend Pinte's soul to god. One or both are to dig the grave. In the next line Bruin goes to put on the stole with an unidentified assistant.

Line 402. Tilander (*Remarques*, p. 11) prefers the reading of C: *couvreture*, "a place covered with trees." It is true that Pinte's grave is beneath a tree.

Line 429. This formula, *Qui lors veïst Pintein plorer . . . Molt grant pitie l'en poïst prendre*, echoes "La Vie de Saint Alexis" (*Qui donc li vit son grant duel demener . . . N'i out si dur ne l'estoust plorer*, ed. Gaston, Paris), the death of Olivier (*Ki lui vedist sarrazins desmembrer . . .*, ed. Jenkins), and many another great moment. Cf. Branch Va, lines 699ff.

Line 431. At this point Chanteclere presumably faints.

Line 441. As in the *Chanson de Roland* when the extreme concern expressed for and by the ambassador to the supposedly pacific Marsile shows that no one really believed that the pagans wanted peace, King Noble would not have said that Bruin would be in no danger if he, in fact, believed it. Such details, of course, enhance the prestige of the fox.

Line 445. All the animals, as feudal barons, necessarily ride, and the skill of the individual poets is much tested by having them do so without becoming grotesque. The author of Branch I is a master at this and can even go so far as to mention that the cat rides sidesaddle.

Line 463. The dog, Roenel, as in Branch II, makes Ysengrin a useful ally.

Line 472. Renard's relationship with Tibert is particularly interesting. The cat is the beast most like the fox, being playful and seeming to enjoy, as we see in Branch II, matching wits with Renard, who respects Tibert's claws and avoids irritating him when they are within reach of each other. Despite his caution, Renard ends up in a trap he had hoped to spring on the cat. We do not find Tibert actually taking Renard's part in court proceedings, although he is at one point allied with Grinbert. In Branch Va he is specifically mentioned on the opposing side (*Tybers . . . Qui Renart het*, lines 1069–1070). Grinbert, Renard's one real ally, is cautious, even crafty, and anything but playful.

Lines 480–481. A nice juxtaposition of the fox's den, into which the beast certainly could not fit, and the fortress of Maupertuis which Noble and a mighty army would one day besiege.

Line 522. Literally: "burning coals."

Line 523. C (line 543) has a comma after this line, so that those who hang on to their bread are the seneschals and cooks. C's *preu* in line 546, a better rhyme where Martin has *peu*, gives the lords and the thieves the same good food on their tables. It is unclear whether both groups or only the "sergants" are to be burned at the stake together *en un ré* instead of Martin's *et venté*.

Line 526. Tilander (*Lexique*, p. 38) suggests that this mold was a round and plump one, *coing* meaning also "quince."

Line 537. Bruin's Latin is less than ideal.

Lines 566–574. This dialogue, with its short, lively phrases, seems to reflect the style of Chrétien de Troyes.

Line 599. Martin's line 599, *Maudite soit sa vie tote*, is translated in line 603.

Line 611. Another way of saying "may he be damned."

Line 623. Rey-Flaud and Eskénazi, *Le Roman de Renard*, Librairie Honoré Champion, Paris, 1978, translate *poires moles* in the sense of bringing rotten fruit to the sick.

Line 627. *li vilains.*

Line 724. The text reads *Renart t'a mort*, but Bruin's death, like most apparent fatalities in the *Roman*, is not permanent. (See Branch I, line 1208.)

Line 756. "Saint Martin's bird."

Line 777. "Welcomme" is in the text, rhyming with "Rome."

Line 779. Saint-Jacques de Compostela in Spain, a famous destination for pilgrims. If Tibert was listening carefully, he must have found this hospitable speech somewhat disquieting, Renard having no special love for pilgrims and Tibert, in any case, not being one.

Lines 804–808. Tibert begins by asking for poultry, but in the lines that follow, the translation is somewhat less ambiguous than the text. Tibert enters the trap in direct response to Renard's telling him where he had stored away the hens he couldn't eat. In line 1074, however, he is said to have been looking for rats.

Line 864. Such sport as, to follow the text more closely, one would have with someone who is crazy. *Li gorpilz est tenus por fou.*

Line 878. *Et Tybert jete avant les danz.*

Lines 956–959. This passage is clearer and perhaps more logical in C, where it is Renard who, fearing attack and hearing noises in his house, closes himself in and waits to see who is coming.

Line 962. *pont torneiz.*

Line 969. *Desoz li ploie deus cosins* (as opposed to C's *li mist desoz lui II cousins*) offers an example of the vigorous expressiveness characteristic of Old French verbs.

Line 981. *Prendra ja vostra guerre fin?*

Line 1049. Literally: "like an ass on a bridge."

Line 1059. *De l'ombre de la blanc image*—the melodious *l*'s and vowel sounds make *furmage* an amusing surprise. Foulet (p. 335) suggests that the source of this adventure may be the fable in which Marie de France tells of a fox drinking up the water of a pond to reach the reflection he took for a cheese.

Lines 1065–1068. Ysengrin is tonsured with boiling water in Branch III, and there is another such episode in Branch XIV where the wolf is Primaut, Ysengrin's brother, trapped by his greed in a chapel. C omits the allusion to the wolf as shepherd.

Line 1074. He seemed rather to be expecting poultry.

Line 1088. *Qar je lor toli lor soudees.*

Line 1091. Where Martin (*Lor toli ge lor convenant*) indicates an unspecified way of betraying the enemy armies, C (*lor toli ge lor paiement*) suggests that Renard somehow manages to take the money paid to the mercenary troups (*soudees*) mentioned in both texts.

Line 1107. *romanz.*

Line 1117. "Lord" would be a translation of *chastelain*, not the feminine form given in both texts. But while the wife of a castle-holder might well direct its defense, she would be less likely to lead an attack. Rey-Flaud and Eskénazi suggest *chievetaine.*

Line 1121. "Seven years"–Renard's optimism, or pretended optimism, grows with his speech, in contrast to the "months" mentioned in line 1116. C, however, only goes as far as one year.

Line 1151. *parmi un pleins.*

Line 1177. Literally: "great sin is rushing to attack you" (*certes grant peche te cort sore*).

Line 1190.   Grinbert's mount has been demoted from a charger to a mule.

Line 1191.   Although the punctuation in Martin does not admit of such a reading, it seems more probable that it is Renard, and not his horse, who is afraid of his *seigneur*. C is similar to Martin. In any case it is a nice observation that the reluctance or fear of the rider interferes with the horse's gaits.

Line 1213*ff.*   It is in his arrogant address to the king that Renard particularly recalls Roland, although the effect of Roland's speeches in this tone is to increase the hostility of the other warriors, not his own immediate danger.

Line 1231.   *serf par nature.*

Line 1261–1264.   Literally: "the faith and great loyalty that I've always had for you have maintained life in my body" (*la vie el cors maintenue*).

Line 1266.   Tilander (*Lexique*, p. 8) explains *ne me puis aidier* as a reference to sexual impotence.

Line 1278.   In the thirteenth-century work *La mort le roi Artu*, the Pope sends a message to Arthur to the effect that even if Lancelot and the queen have been caught *in flagrante* they are to be considered innocent because there was no trial.

Line 1290.   *Renardie.*

Line 1302.   *Se nos vers vos nos abessons / Por droit fere et por afetier.*

Line 1310.   *par amor.*

Lines 1432–1433.   The expression *rompre le fétu* which occurs in line 1433 of the text is explained by Tilander (*Remarques*, p. 25) as being derived from a gesture symbolizing the breaking off of homage, but here the meaning is simply that Renard's separation from Noble is to be definitive.

Line 1434.   The canonical hour, *none*, the ninth hour after sunrise. Hence, after noon.

Line 1451.   Renard's offer of "jewels" involves a double meaning indicated by Rey-Flaud and Eskénazi who cite Beroul's *Tristan: O lie faisoie mes joiaus.* This suggestion is adopted by the author of "Le Siège de Maupertuis" who has Renard attack Fiere sexually. Tilander (*Lexique*, p. 94) interprets *joiel* in the same sense.

Lines 1456–1458.   These lines are not very clear, but the implication is that Renard attributes a magical protective power to the ring, or perhaps he simply plans to make improper use of it as a sign of royal authority.

Line 1482. Using C's *morir* in place of Martin's *traïr*.

Line 1505. *Tant voit barons et tantes bestes.*

Line 1521. The Sultan Noradin, who personified the pagan enemy before the time of his successor Saladin. (Foulet, p. 108, says this permits us to date the poem before 1187 and perhaps before 1183.)

Line 1550. Foulet observes that Pierre de Saint-Cloud would not have had the king show so little recognition of his vassals' nobility as to offer to enfranchise their descendants. The translation takes *franc* to mean "noble" but even so it is more of an insult than an incentive.

Line 1574. Short the bitch as in C, rather than *tote la rote* followed by *li autre* in Martin.

Line 1604. "Shady" suggests the furtive aspect of *Percehaie* but not its humorous imitation of *Perceval.*

BRANCH VIII

Line 11. According to Foulet's chronology, this poem was composed some fourteen years after Branch Va, time enough for Renard to begin feeling his age. Bossuat, however, dates it ten years earlier, c. 1180.

Line 38. According to Tilander's explanation of this passage (*Remarques,* p. 26), Renard's habit was to play dead, lying on his back and allowing the hens to peck at him "d'une manière peu délicate."

Line 44. *Une en fis je porter en biere* seems to suggest that carrying the dead hen to Noble's court was Renard's idea, but perhaps he is simply taking as much pride as he could in having been responsible for such an effect.

Line 87. This rare generosity in a peasant of the *Roman* deserves to be noted.

Line 107. Renard presumably considered himself the priest's enemy simply for having lived so unchristian a life, rather than for any more particular cause.

Line 124. *Hersent la bele ma seror,* but "sister" only in a generalized sense.

Line 126. See note to Branch I, lines 1065–1068.

Line 129. The boar's head would have been a delicacy of the dinner table.

Line 132.   Another example of epic accounting.

Line 172.   C adds four lines suggesting that Renard was afraid to travel alone: *il se crient mout de sa pel.*

Line 183.   C has *respons,* "answer," instead of *repos.*

Line 203.   Presumably the first of three days of special supplication preceding Rogation Sunday, the fifth Sunday after Easter.

Line 221.   In the original, this reference to a real sheep's preferences is more deftly accomplished because "grass" is not the rhyming word.

Line 239.   An *archeprestre* named Bernard cannot fail to evoke Bernard of Clairvaux, more convincingly portrayed, however, in Branch VI where he persuades King Noble to send Renard to a monastery rather than hang him.

Line 244.   *Renard le gorpil.*

Line 270.   Foulet (pp. 437–440) discusses the influence of *Ysengrimus* on Branch VIII. *Ysengrimus* involves eight pilgrims, most fleeing human masters who intend to devour them. The resemblances are certainly striking, but the author of the French version is alone responsible for having Renard suggest that the pilgrims spend the night in the wolves' lair (lines 294–295).

Line 276.   This is the forest of the courtly romance where the wanderer will find nothing that is unrelated to his *aventure* (E. Auerbach, *Mimesis,* Doubleday, New York, 1957, p. 119).

Line 294.   Renard's kinsman is called "Primaut" here, a name which seems to have meant nothing to Belin and Bernard but which the medieval reader may have recognized as that of a wolf, if not specifically Ysengrin, since it was the name given to the wolf in Branch XIV (c. 1178). In Branch VIII, however, the wolf is alternately called "Primaut" and "Ysengrin." The translation eliminates "Primaut" and with him an unnecessary source of confusion. It should be said, however, that Renard, in so naming the owner of the house, may have been giving Bernard and Belin a chance to recognize a danger which, given their timid natures, they would probably not have been as willing to risk as he was himself.

Line 300.   C has *son art* instead of *son barat* and does not identify the menace; that is, he omits lines 301 and 302.

Line 324.   A *pertuis* or spy hole (Tilander, *Remarques,* pp. 89–90).

Line 435.   *esquacha.*

Line 467.   *Outree, outree!,* "onward!," the traditional cry of pilgrims.

A Brief Account Of Branches Not Translated

BRANCH V   Much influenced by *Ysengrimus*, this branch has Renard, still convalescing, meet Ysengrin who attacks him and then is afraid he has killed him. To his relief Renard comes to, they are reconciled, and they steal a ham which Ysengrin manages to devour without any help from Renard. The latter, too weak to object, leaves Ysengrin and tries to satisfy his hunger in some other way but fails in his attempts to catch first a rat and then a cricket. The wolf is chased by a pack of dogs, and Renard watches from safety.

BRANCH XV   In a style worthy of Pierre de Saint-Cloud, but not his work (Foulet, pp. 251–256), Tibert cheats Renard of a sausage they stole together. Two priests, seeing the cat perched on top of a cross, decide how they will share the profits from his skin, but Tibert claws one of them to such effect that he falls off his horse which then serves the cat as a means of escape. Humans have major roles in this branch, and the protagonist is Tibert rather than Renard. Ysengrin does not appear.

BRANCH III   Seeing a cart heavily loaded with fish, Renard plays dead and soon finds himself added to the pile of merchandise. He eats as much as he can, wraps strings of eels around his neck, jumps off, and runs home. Soon the odor of roasting eels attracts Ysengrin who, as if drunk with hunger and hope, allows himself to believe that Maupertuis has become a monastery in which only the tonsured can dine. The operation is carried out with boiling water, after which Ysengrin's initiation rites include spending a night with his tail through a hole in a frozen pond. In the morning some peasants find him trapped, and he is lucky to escape having lost only his tail. Foulet demonstrates convincingly that these episodes form a unity and that they are derived from *Ysengrimus.*

BRANCH IV   Renard is trapped in the well of a monastery from which he escapes by persuading Ysengrin that he is dead and is in a heaven wonderfully provided with food. Ysengrin jumps into the well's upper bucket (a particularity of this telling of the familiar story which Foulet, p. 308, attributes to Pierre Alphonse's *Disciplina Clericalis*) and finds himself at the bottom where he is discovered by the monks and barely escapes with his life.

BRANCH XIV   The first part involves Tibert and Renard in various escapades during one of which the cat cheats the fox of Chanteclere, who had been seized yet again, by asking whether Renard has a good hold on him. Renard opens his mouth to answer. Then Primaut, replacing his brother Ysengrin, accompanies Renard to a monastery where holy wafers and wine are the attraction. Later Primaut tries Renard's trick of playing dead to attract the attention of fishmongers, but is less successful than the fox. Renard leads Primaut into a larder where he eats so much he can't get out the way he had entered but eventually escapes by biting its owner. Further alliance between Primaut and Renard ends with Primaut caught by his paw in a trap he was persuaded to believe a holy martyr's tomb.

BRANCH Ia   The Siege of Maupertuis. While the members of the king's army, resigned to a lengthy campaign, are all asleep one night, Renard attaches their tails to trees and treats Fiere with no respect for her queenly dignity. The beasts are liberated by the snail who cuts the ropes with his sword, and Renard is saved from execution only by the arrival of his wife and sons with money for his ransom. A family of rats intervenes, in the manner of Pinte and Chanteclere of Branch I, but Renard nonetheless escapes, perhaps because the generous Fiere had given him a protective talisman.

BRANCH Ib   Apparently inspired by an Indian tale, this branch has Renard fall into a vat of yellow dye which makes him unrecognizable. He plays the part of a Breton *jongleur* and, having acquired a viol with the help of Ysengrin, offers to play at the wedding of Hermeline who, thinking herself a widow, is about to marry one of Grinbert's nephews. The new husband is lured into a trap and devoured by dogs, after which Renard chases both Hermeline and the equally unfaithful Hersent. These two quarrel violently, are separated by a pilgrim, and Hermeline goes home to be reconciled with Renard.

B R A N C H   X   Noble is so ill that he agrees to take Renard as his doctor. The fox's remedies, totally successful, include Ysengrin's skin and Bricemer's horns. Renard is rewarded with two castles and an imposing escort. The source of the tale is Aesop, but the mid-tenth-century *Ecbasis Captivi* gives it greater scope, and it has well over a thousand lines in *Ysengrimus* (Foulet, p. 371–373).

B R A N C H   V I   Renard is again summoned to appear in court and agrees to a duel with Ysengrin, which the latter wins. The intervention of a venerable priest named Bernard saves the fox from hanging, but he ends up in a monastery where the diet seems a fate worse than death. Finally banished from holy orders, Renard regains Maupertuis and his own dinner table.

B R A N C H   V I I   Adventures clearly inspired by their predecessors involve Renard's love of confession. This time, having admitted eating the four children of his confessor, a kite, he ends by eating the confessor as well.

B R A N C H   I X   Renard helps a peasant, one Liétard, save his ox from Bruin, who ends up as salted meat in the peasant's larder. Instead of giving Renard the cock he had promised in exchange, Liétard sets the dogs on him and he arrives at Maupertuis minus his tail. Later Renard catches Liétard poaching on the count's lands, the penalty for which is death. Renard takes such advantage of this, despite Liétard's efforts to outmaneuver him, that very little remains in the peasant's barnyard at the end of the story. The author, who styles himself a village priest, is interested in peasant life in which animals are sources of food, and aristocrats are distant and threatening humans.

B R A N C H   X I I   A rather disagreeable tale of another alliance between Tibert and Renard, who become acting priests of a Norman parish, to Tibert's regret.

B R A N C H   X I   A long but mediocre series of adventures including one in which Renard helps a worried sparrow by devouring her young. The branch is primarily concerned with the fox, now a widower, who manages to take Noble's place as king and husband of Fiere. The animal-aristocrats of the early tales are here reduced to contributing only the names of characters in a poor imitation of epic and romance.

BRANCH XVI   The author pretends to be Pierre de Saint-Cloud and returns to the style of Branch II, but without Pierre's inspiration. He includes an account of the division of the lion's spoils.

BRANCH XVII   The animals, whether killed in preceding tales or still surviving, assemble at Noble's court for the feast of the martyred Copee. Renard, playing chess with Ysengrin, bets a most cherished part of his person and loses. His death is celebrated with solemnities and gaiety. Bernard the high priest pronounces the funeral oration. But when the burial begins, Renard leaps out of his grave and seizes Chanteclere, but is captured. He accuses the cock of having tried to bury him alive. The result is a duel that ends when Renard plays dead again, so convincingly that he succeeds in biting off the leg of a crow who is pecking at his body. Back in Maupertuis he knows that this time he cannot answer the king's demand that he appear in court, and Grinbert reports that Renard is dead and has been buried by his grieving widow. There is even a tombstone as proof, providentially belonging to a peasant named Renard. Foulet (pp. 472–473) remarks that this narrative returns to the clerical humor of *Ysengrimus* from which Pierre de Saint-Cloud had so happily departed, but the author of Branch XVII does give Renard a death that truly suits his authentic style.

Bibliography

Batany, Jean. *Scènes et Coulisses du Roman de Renart*. Paris: SEDES. 1989.

Best, T.W. *Reynard the Fox*. TWAS, 673. Boston and New York: Twayne. 1983.

Bloch, R. Howard. *Medieval French Literature and the Law*. Berkeley: University of California Press. 1977.

Bossuat, Robert. *Le Roman de Renart*. Paris: Hatier. 1967.

Dufournet, Jean, ed. *Le Roman de Renard* (Martin). Paris: Garnier-Flammarion. 1970.

Dufournet, Jean, ed/tr. *Le Roman de Renart*, 2 vols. Paris: Garnier Flammarion. 1985.

Flinn, John. *Le Roman de Renart dans la littérature française et dans les littératures étrangères au moyen âge*. University of Toronto Press. 1963.

Foulet, Lucien. *Le Roman de Renart*. Paris: Librairie Honoré Champion. 1968.

Fukomoto, N. Harano, N. Suzuki, S. ed. *Le Roman de Renart*. Tokyo: France Tosho. 1983–85.

Graven, Jean. *Le Procès criminel du Roman de Renart*. Genève: Georg & Cie. 1950.

Lodge, Anthony and Varty, Kenneth. *The Earliest Branches of Le Roman de Renart*. New Alyth: Lochee. 1989.

Reinardus (Yearbook of the International Reynard Society). vols 1 and 2 Grave: Alfa. 1988, 1989; vol 3, Amsterdam: Benjamins. 1990.

Rey-Flaud, Henri, and Eskénazi, André. *Le Roman de Renart*. Paris: Librarie Honoré Champion. 1978.

Roques, Mario, ed. *Le Roman de Renart* (Cangé). 3 vols. Paris: Librarie Honoré Champion. 1972–74.

Scheidegger, Jean R. *Le Roman de Renart ou le texte de la dérision*. Genève: Droz. 1989.

Tilander, Gunnar. *Remarques sur Le Roman de Renart*. Göteborg: Elanders Boktryckeri Aktiebolag. 1923.

CPSIA information can be obtained at www.ICGtesting.com
224513LV00001B/4/A